Only Human

Centre for
Faith and Spirituality
Loughborough University

ONLY HUMAN

Don Cupitt

SCM PRESS LTD

334 02235 5

First published 1985
by SCM Press Ltd
26–30 Tottenham Road, London N1 4BZ

Typeset at The Spartan Press Ltd
Lymington, Hants
and printed in Great Britain by
Billing and Sons Ltd, Worcester

For John

Contents

Introduction

This is — or aims to be — a new kind of theological book. It starts not from doctrine or scripture but from the rise of those sciences that bear most directly on the questions of human nature and the human condition. The idea is to find out what religious possibilities there may be in the emergent modern vision of our situation.

A generation ago people could still identify something called the Christian doctrine of man,[1] which had been highly influential in Western culture for fifteen centuries; but of all the branches of theology it had become one of the most badly damaged. At least half of its main themes came straight from Genesis, and had been undermined by biblical criticism and natural science. In addition, its chief architect, Augustine, had been finally repudiated by the mainstream of Western culture since the end of the seventeenth century.

So there is a gap to be filled, but this book offers no straightforward replacements for the beliefs that history has eroded. It is a hard thing to say, but the trouble with the old theology is not that its propositions were difficult to verify, nor an insufficiency of evidence for them. The trouble is more serious than that. It is that not just these particular theological beliefs, but all dogmatic theological beliefs as such, belong to a world that is gone, and now can no more be put to effective use in our own world than can the myths of some exotic tribe. They are historically intelligible, but if I try personally to get hold of them I find that they are so intolerably vague, slippery and confused that I can get no purchase on them and am not able to tie them in with other beliefs or to make them do any useful work.

Suppose that someone writing a textbook of psychology is told to integrate the Scientologists' beliefs into his text. He really and truly wishes to comply with this instruction, but he finds that even with the best will in the world it simply cannot be done. *That* is the difficulty that we are in. Maybe it is bad news, but shooting the messenger who brings it will not help.

So the Christian doctrine of man will not in these pages be reinterpreted or pruned or modernized, nor will it be replaced by any new set of doctrines. I have no 'theological anthropology' to present, and no new doctrines to replace the old ones, because the task is not to substitute new and up-to-date doctrines for old and worn-out ones, but to learn a new kind of religious existence that is no longer based on doctrines in the old way.

For the same reason I have no 'philosophical anthropology' to offer, either. I am not, even in the most modest way, attempting a general characterization of the human condition that mixes existentialism, psychology and a little metaphysics. That kind of philosophy is no more than the ghost of theology, and it is as dead now as is doctrinal belief.

Where then shall we find firm ground on which to stand? We take a hint from Foucault: since what you are reading is a literary text, the one thing that we cannot self-consistently be sceptical about is language itself. There is, at least, a record of debates and controversies about human origins and human nature. So we draw our materials from the early history of these modern sciences which bear most directly on the human situation: geology and biology in Part I, psychology in Part II, social anthropology in Part III, and comparative religion in Part IV. By anchoring our discussions in these fields, where there are at least real texts we can point to and real controversies we can study, we hope to keep sane and avoid folly and eccentricity. If this can be done in a religious book, it will be no small achievement.

In each area I am inevitably highly selective, picking the topics on which, as it seems to me, there is something interesting to be said. I can claim no more objectivity for my selection than may have been gained by a dozen years of lecturing on and teaching these subjects.

The analogy, then, is that as Foucault wrote his philosophy through the history of ideas, so we are attempting to write theology indirectly, through a kind of critical reflection on the history of ideas. We search for the religious significance of the modern human situation. I believe that other styles of religious writing which interpret scripture, or which develop a tradition, or which reflect on and articulate religious life and experience or whatever, are all now unsatisfactory. They seem to be too vague and self-indulgent. Something tougher is needed.

However, I repeat that we will not be arriving at any new doctrinal beliefs, so those who still equate religious faith with holding doctrinal beliefs to be true are going to be disappointed. In order to keep sane and avoid arbitrariness we agreed to stick to language and to the history of human discourses, an agreement that committed us to the modern post-metaphysical way of thinking.

This new way of thinking is radically language-centred and man-centred. Once we have become fully conscious of our languages and other forms of symbolic communication as sign-systems through which everything thinkable or knowable is mediated, then we see that there can be no sense in the idea of transcending language. It was clumsy of me even to put it into words in the last sentence. How can there be 'words' not themselves part of language, that we can use to state the relation of language to 'reality', or whatever it is that we naively imagine to stand beyond language? And when we grasp this we become dizzy, for we see for the first time that the human realm is now absolutely alone. There is no sense in the idea that there could be any guidelines or reference-points external to it that might help us to get it into perspective. That is why it is so hard to say what the human situation is: there is no longer anything else with which to compare and contrast it. As in a late Beckett play, the world is just voices, talk, meanings, symbols.

The human world, which is the world of language, is alone: I sometimes call this new situation 'anthropomonism'. Try its implications for the question of death: it means that our life is what it is, it is bounded, it is all there is for us, and outside it there is nothing at all, not even nothingness. So, come back to the human world. You can no more step out of it than you can step out of the Universe of the modern cosmologists. Be content with what is.

We need something like the Buddha's Fourfold Negation to explain the point: life outside this life is not anything that can intelligibly be either affirmed, or denied, or both affirmed and denied, or neither affirmed nor denied. Outside life there is not even nothing. Stop thinking in such ways, cure yourself of trying to talk nonsense! Understand that language is all, life is all, and forget about trying to step outside, for there is no such step that could conceivably be taken.

However, even the last two paragraphs were still deeply false, because they were still anti-metaphysical rather than completely post-metaphysical; and my problem is to get religious belief (and myself, and you) into this new completely post-metaphysical world without subverting myself. For the more I say, 'Forget metaphysics, forget the illusions of transcendence, forget the absurd idea that, human, you can step out of the human realm, forget the absurd idea that language can transcend language, and return to the human realm, for it is all there could possibly be and you have not lost anything that you could ever conceivably have possessed . . . ' – the more I say all this, the more I harp on and nourish the very sentiments that I am trying to persuade you (and myself) to forget completely. I must not denounce nostalgia, but rather cure it.

The most intellectually-correct and consistent techniques for me to use would be those of Jacques Derrida.[2] He is the modern Kierkegaard. As Kierkegaard had to use stratagems to subvert Hegelianism, so Derrida has to use stratagems to subvert the pretensions and the realist illusions of Western reason, and to coax us through to the new way of thinking. A similar deconstruction of all false, nostalgic, otherworldly and metaphysical styles in theology is now needed in order to purify religion.

However, the English-speaking world probably has nobody to write such a text and nobody to read it, so instead we will proceed in our typically muddled English manner, which, we like to think, gets us there in the end just the same. May I add two final comments to obviate misunderstanding? I use the word 'man' to signify the species, humankind, female and male alike: *Anthropos, homo*. There is not much choice in the matter, for it is the established term in theology, where 'person' carries a number of special technical associations. Secondly, I do not here replace or repeat, but in the main simply assume the views about God, Christ and the nature of religious language that I have been advancing since late 1979. Just before beginning this book I wrote five short articles for *The Listener*, to be published while *The Sea of Faith* was being transmitted on television, and they are now reprinted here with the kind agreement of the editor. They may serve as a (perhaps rather bald) summary.

I am concerned that many people feel that such a position is somehow impoverished. Really, it is not so. Let us suggest that what is here contained, in the Appendix and in the main text, is analogous to what used to be called 'natural theology'. Then the 'revealed theology', with all its rich symbolic, mythical and emotional content, is added by the actual living of the religious life within our own particular tradition of faith. The philosophy of religion cannot supply more than a bare, rather intimidating skeleton. Practice, practice and only practice, can put flesh on these bones.

Don Cupitt

Cambridge
October 1984

PART I

A LIFE IN TIME

1

Natural History

In 1755 the first modern theory of cosmic evolution was published in the philosopher Kant's *Universal Natural History and Theory of the Heavens*. It outlines a nebular hypothesis, clearly recognizes a plurality of galaxies, and speaks in terms of millions of years. In 1965 Penzias and Wilson reported their discovery of the 3°K cosmic microwave radiation background. This radiation was at once recognized as a surviving trace of the early universe, and therefore as clinching evidence that there had indeed been an early universe, from which the present state of the universe has evolved.

Two centuries separated these events, a period in which people gradually became accustomed to the strange idea that the Earth, that life, that indeed the entire Universe, has a natural history.[1]

During this same period the very phrase 'natural history' has had a curious ambiguity. When Buffon published the first volumes of his *Natural History* in 1749, he seemed at first to be using the phrase in its received sense of a purely descriptive survey of some field of natural phenomena, without any connotations of evolutionary change or narrative. In this archaic sense we may still to this day describe a bird book or a Flora as a work of natural history. But Buffon's encyclopaedia was to be laid out in linear sequence – the solar system, the Earth, the human race, the animal and plant kingdoms – and by the time he had issued his *Theory of the Earth* it was already apparent that his great work was to be a non-theological narrative history. Natural history in the old non-temporal and purely descriptive sense was changing into an historical explanatory theory of Nature's evolution. The theologians of the Sorbonne soon put a stop to these speculations, but a quarter of a century later Buffon managed to return to them, publishing in 1778 his *Epochs of Nature*.

Buffon's Epochs of Nature are still residually theological, or even mythical: for one thing, he has seven of them corresponding to the seven days of Creation in Genesis, and for another, he still clings to the ancient mythic idea of a primeval Ocean that in his third epoch covers the whole globe. Nevertheless, Buffon's account aims to be naturalistic and to be supported by mathematical calculations, and that is the important thing.

This change in the meaning of the phrase 'natural history' is just one indication that the rise of our modern historical sciences of nature was part of a larger shift in language, in ways of thinking and in our culture as a whole. During the key period – roughly 1750–1860 – neither 'science' nor 'religion' existed in a pure state as self-contained activities. In fact, they never do: as is always the case, the abstractions that people call 'science' and 'religion' were simply two overlapping areas in a cultural totality that was itself in revolutionary change.

The point is vital. Neither science nor religion has a fixed essence of its own. The forms they take at any given time are determined by the mentality or the system of thought then prevailing.

Michael Foucault (1927–84), in his book *Les Mots et les Choses* (*The Order of Things*, 1966) introduced the word *episteme* to describe the system of thought characteristic of a particular historical epoch. *Episteme* is a wider term than the term *paradigm*, popularized by T. S. Kuhn. What Foucault means by it is best shown by explaining how he describes the change of *episteme* that was taking place in Western culture around the time of the French Revolution.

In what Foucault calls 'classical' thinking, of the sort that prevailed from Descartes to Linnaeus and after, a space is set up within which objects are ordered, classified and anatomized. Science, organized knowledge, sets out to explain the world as a stable and harmonious system. The operation of forces is always seen as tending to restore equilibrium and to maintain the proper balance of things, rather than bring about permanent change.

By contrast, in 'modern' thinking, pioneered by such figures as Vico, Herder and Buffon, and increasingly dominant after Kant and the French Revolution, time rather than space becomes fundamental. Conflict between persons, States, ideas and forces now comes to be seen as leading to progressive change and development. The old Aristotelian logic of things and their properties and of fixed kinds tends to be replaced by the new Hegelian logic of process. Everywhere, ideas of organism, function, the will, labour, struggle, revolution, progressive self-expression and unfolding self-realization become dominant.

The best single example of the effect of the change of episteme is the transformation of the human self.[2] For Descartes the self had been a self-perspicuous thinking spiritual substance set outside physical nature, which it observes. But the Romantic self that came into being from the 1780s is entirely different. It is no longer a fixed substance but a process of becoming or, as the Germans say, *Bildung*. This new kind of self develops itself by its own self-expression, battling its way out of the relatively formless darkness of unconsciousness towards progressively clearer consciousness, individuality and freedom.

Corresponding shifts affect all branches of knowledge. For example, with Adam Smith there begins the idea, now utterly familiar to us, that the operation of economic forces tends to produce, not stability, but economic growth. Or again, with Hegel and Schleier-macher Christianity's relation to time is reversed. In the older way of thinking the primitive perfection of the faith has a strong tendency to become corrupted as the generations pass. Time causes decay, and periodic reformations are needed to restore the primitive purity of faith. But in the new way of thinking Christianity is actually improved by the passage of time, as the historical process brings about the growth and the ever more complete realization of the Christian Idea.

The upshot of all this is that nobody then (that is, around 1750–1860) was able to see the issues 'pure'. I mean that, as geology and biology were gradually historicized, everyone was indeed aware that something very important for religious thought, and for our whole sense of what we are and of our place in the world, was going on. But nobody saw the issues in a tidy way, in terms of the logical relations between clearly-defined scientific theories and clearly-defined religious doctrines. It was not at all like that: rather, the issues were seen in a large, cloudy and emotional way that was moulded chiefly by the general change in episteme that was going on.

We have to say something of this kind in order to explain why an intelligent man like John Ruskin could feel that he heard the death-knell of Christianity in every tap of the geologist's hammer, while yet he never spells out to us precisely *how* geological discoveries are supposed to falsify important religious beliefs. In retrospect, it seems odd that so many writers were convinced that the entire Christian scheme must founder if the opening chapters of Genesis were not scientifically accurate. Why, we may ask ourselves, were they so illogical? And the answer appears to be that scientific theories and religious beliefs are always culturally clothed, in such a way that at that time (say, the 1820s to 1840s) people perceived the advances in geology as signs and portents of a larger change of *episteme* that, they thought, was irresistibly removing the whole world-view of traditional Christianity as they understood it. We live at a time when people take a cool view of geology, and moreover after the end of the great nineteenth-century modern episteme. It was destroyed, Foucault thought, by Nietzsche, even though its ghost lingers yet in the popular mind. Be that as it may, we are much cooler about the issues now. At the time, the Vatican and Karl Marx were agreed in reacting to Darwin's theory of evolution as if it were really a political theory. To the Roman Catholic Church darwinism was a typical expression of the noxious secular and anti-clerical spirit of the period, and Marx liked its progressivism but misliked the overtones of Manchester-Liberal economics. We may be surprised, and wonder why Rome and Karl Marx did not assess darwinism simply as a scientific theory, but at the time darwinism was wrapped up in an episteme – one that affected Darwin himself as much as anyone else. We can pretend to assess darwinism purely scientifically only because for us it has been broken out of its original episteme by the latter's decay.

This prompts the thought that perhaps for us it is now repackaged in another episteme of which we are largely unaware.

The implications are worrying. Consider the origins of modern economics again. People have long recognized that there are such things as market forces; and there was once a generation that assumed that these forces must operate, in a Newtonian way, to keep the economy balanced and stable. As they believed, so, approximately, their world was. But then along came a new generation who believed that all forces operate in a dialectical way to bring about, through conflict, progressive change and development. And lo, it was so.

None of the facts had changed; or at least, they had not changed very much. But a deep, pervasive and very mysterious change in people's assumptions had taken place, a change of a sort that, it seems, can be recognized only with hindsight, and which nobody is yet able fully to explain. The reasons why 'mentalities' change are unknown: Hegel's way of explaining cultural change is itself part of a dead episteme. Today it seems that the wind blows, and a selection from the range of ideas that are possible in this age of ours passes through our heads – and we have not the least idea where they have come from or whither they are going. All we can say with some confidence is that it seems that in any one period only a certain range of thoughts are possible; that it is very hard to grasp the constraints that limit what can be thought in one's own period; and that we do not know what the reasons for cultural change are.

In the past moralistic reasons for historical change were given in history books. Why did the Reformation happen? 'Reformation' implies a preceding state of corruption: therefore the pre-Reformation church *was* corrupt. But if the best index of the spiritual life of an age is the quality of its art, then this supposed explanation must be wrong, because late-medieval German art is of such superlatively high religious quality that it makes the Reformation appear to be more like a disaster. And Foucault's insight is that any kind of moralizing about cultural change is to be avoided.

Certain other great constraints on our thinking have been recognized by Marx and Freud and others. But the ones presently under discussion (our ignorance of why what can be thought or done in any period is limited, and of why cultural change takes place at all), are particularly galling and difficult. I feel myself in the toils of an opponent who is invisible and whom I cannot make visible, and he threatens me with severe scepticism unless I can discover his secret.

Awareness of the episteme-problem began in the nineteenth century when it became obvious that the same great conflict between two very different mentalities – conservative and progressive, Right and Left – underlay dozens of different disputes.[3] Here is a list of some of the main ones, with the pessimistic conservative position first and the optimistic liberal one second. Imagine that the date is about 1850.

Tory *versus* Whig.

The conservation of an established way of thinking and body of knowledge *versus* the progressive enlargement of knowledge by critical thinking and free enquiry.

An infallible Bible and church, and immutable dogma *versus* biblical criticism, free religious enquiry and progressive religious development.

Human nature basically anarchic and needing to be disciplined by strong social institutions *versus* human nature basically good, if liberated from the shackles of obsolete and oppressive social institutions.

Degradationism (i.e., history a record of decline from the primitive paradisal perfection) *versus* progressionism (i.e., history a record of the ascent of man from his lowly origins).

Eternal and unchangeable intellectual and moral standards *versus* historical relativity, with change and progress not merely in the degree of conformity to standards, but in the very standards that are acknowledged.

'The religious sanction – that is, the fear of God's judgment – is necessary to maintain social order' *versus* 'On the contrary, there are strong moral objections to judgment and to Hell'.

Schopenhauer's conservative atheist pessimism: doubts about the status of the moral realm, and fears that human existence is ultimately futile in an amoral universe *versus* liberal optimism and historicism, with the faith that society and even the cosmos can be progressively moralized.

Catastrophism and a personal interventionist God *versus* Uniformitarianism and naturalism or deism.

Right-wing malthusianism: 'People must stand on their own feet; too much welfare will pauperize and demoralize them' *versus* belief in the power of structural reform and collective action steadily to diminish social evils.

But we could go on for pages likes this: let us take it as established that in the early and middle nineteenth century conflicts within science, and conflicts between science and religion, were interwoven with and embedded in wider conflicts of a political and epistemic kind in society. To put it in the crudest terms, in geology catastrophism was Tory and uniformitarianism was liberal: in biology darwinism was a *New Statesman*-type doctrine, whereas anti-darwinism was *Spectator*ish. The conflict between classical-traditional and modern epistemes worked itself out in a struggle between typically conservative and typically liberal attitudes that extended through many spheres of life – politics, ethics, religion, education, scientific theory, and so on.

Although the tendency of the age was towards the long-term victory of the liberal package of attitudes and beliefs, liberalism never wholly vanquished conservatism until Nietzsche (or, if you prefer to have a slightly later marker, until the First World War) destroyed the intellectual foundations of both of them.

Nietzsche did it by pointing out, with the utmost clarity and force, the conclusions to which the critical thinking which is our principal cultural achievement must lead. Critical thinking, making us aware of the way – or rather, the many ways – in which we ourselves pattern and interpret our own experience, must in the end lead us to see that there is no such fixed cosmic order of things as the conservatives believed in, nor any objective guarantee of progress towards a world-Goal such as the marxists and liberals believed in, nor any moral world-order such as they both believed in. There is not any Reality or Truth in the old sense; there are only the endlessly varied visions and values that human beings project out upon the flux in order to give their lives a kind of meaning. We constructed all the world-views, we made all the theories. They are ours, and we are not accountable to them. They depend on us, not we on them.

So the twentieth century, the Nietzschean age, became a century of play. Neither marxism nor conservatism had metaphysical foundations any longer. They, like all other faiths and ideologies, had simply to be chosen and affirmed gratuitously and their relative 'truth' could be assessed and compared only immanently and pragmatically. That is why we make such extensive use of novels, films and plays: these imaginative fictions make excellent testbeds. We use them to 'run' a particular way of life, character-type, moral principle or whatever, simulating the way it works out in practice, in life. No world-view, faith or ideology whatever is objectively anchored in and guaranteed by the nature of things, in the sense that human beings once believed in, for there is no such nature of things. But it does not follow that none of our beliefs is more rational than any other; only, that we must now test our beliefs immanently in terms of their coherence with each other, the way they work out in life, the sense they enable us to make of life, and their fecundity – the extent to which they open up new hypotheses and creative possibilities.

So in what follows we shall not be dogmatic about either scientific theories or religious beliefs. The age of dogmatism is over, and the world is in fact not the poorer but the richer in consequence. We shall be reviewing the history of ideas, the movement of mental life, and in particular the ways in which the new historical sciences of nature, life, man and society have been changing our sense of ourselves.

Our ultimate aim is religious. After the astonishing developments of the last two centuries, it is time to attempt a new religious appraisal of our human condition.

The great thinkers of continental Europe call this enterprise 'philosophical anthropology', the classic works of Sartre and Heidegger being examples of the *genre*. But I suggest that the method of such works was too abstract. Much better to attempt something humbler, clearer and more consistent with the character of our Nietzschean age, namely an archaeology of the modern self. We will get a sense of what we are by reviewing the story of how we got to where we are. The rise of the sciences of life, man and society, and the great controversies and spiritual struggles along the way, will show us how we have become what we are and supply us with materials with which to work. Thus we will anchor our enquiry in the only reality we can be sure of, the history of human discourses.

But, I repeat, our aim is an adequate modern religious self-understanding, the word 'religious' standing for the finality and ethical ultimacy of the enquiry we are to pursue.

2

Natural Theology

The eighteenth century, according to the standard account, was a period when many popular writers appealed strongly to reason and to nature, to natural religion and natural theology. But their conception of the natural order was static and non-developmental. The new historical sciences of geology and biology therefore had to fight it. They did so, and won – with the result that religion ever since has lacked much of its old breadth of empirical rationality and instead has become increasingly pietistic, leaning on tradition and on authority rather than being firmly anchored in the world of fact.

That account is not wholly incorrect, but we will qualify it a great deal, and in the end turn it on its head. Natural theology was first invented by Plato, who in Book X of the *Laws* argued that a certain body of religious truths could be demonstrated purely by reason. The Roman writer Varro further distinguished three kinds of theology: the poetical, which consists of the myths told by the poets; the civil, by which is meant the state cult, maintained by the authorities in the interests of public order; and finally, natural theology, which is simply that branch of the philosophy of nature or reality which deals with the gods.[4] Varro's account suggests that a rational person should be sceptical about myths and about civic religion, and should believe only in natural theology.

However, when Christianity arrived and took over the heritage of Greek philosophy, it shifted the emphasis. The distinction was now between Greek philosophy and Judaeo-Christian scriptures, be-

tween natural theology and revealed theology, the latter being alone
capable of leading a person to salvation. Natural theology did the
useful job of establishing a universal human capacity to understand
the language of revelation. In effect, every human being possessed or
could possess enough preliminary knowledge of God, the moral law,
and the prospect of the Last Judgment to have a strong personal
interest in seizing and appropriating the truths of revelation; but it
was scarcely usual in the medieval centuries to suppose that there
could be a complete working natural religion.

From the sixteenth century, however, the voyages of exploration
were gradually making people more aware of other religions and
cultures beyond Christendom. The new realization that there are a
variety of local religions scattered across the face of the one Earth
brought back Varro's old contrast between the varied local civic
cults and the one universal natural theology. So from the 1620s Lord
Herbert of Cherbury was teaching in advanced circles in Paris that
the true universal or 'catholic' church is the invisible church of all
those people of goodwill around the world who believe in the great
'common notions' or universal rational truths of natural theology.[5]

Herbert goes further, and in a direction that makes him indeed the
Father of Deism, for he asserts the sufficiency of natural religion. His
great common notions include the traditional items – God, the duty
of worship and the Last Judgment – together with a new insistence
on the sufficiency of virtue. The correct way to worship God is to live
a good life, and our vices and crimes can be effaced by simple
repentance, restitution and amendment of life. So we do not in fact
need a mediator and the assistance of supernatural Grace. No special
revelation of saving truth is required; the practice of natural religion
really is by itself sufficient to lead us to salvation. That is Deism.

The church's theologians could scarcely be expected to endorse
this doctrine; so, in writers such as Samuel Clarke (The Arian),
Robert Jenkin and Joseph Butler we find, after the main doctrines of
natural theology have been expounded, that we are presented with a
bridging passage that leads us towards revealed theology.[6]

The teaching contained in this bridging passage is vital to the
whole argument. It runs as follows: to be saved one must be free from
sin, but sin pervades the whole of human life and we are not able to
free ourselves from it. Without supernatural help we cannot gain
salvation. It is therefore highly desirable that we should be given a
special revelation of saving truth. But this makes it *a priori* probable

that the God of natural theology, who is known to be wise and benevolent, will in fact have already bestowed such a revelation upon us. Where is it to be found? – And now we may consider the evidences of Christianity: the beauty of Christ's moral teaching, the miracles wrought by and in him, and the prophecies fulfilled in him.

The point is made: eighteenth-century apologetics required that God's goodness be provable in natural theology, in order to make plausible the remarkable idea of a special revelation from God to bale us out. But at the same time there was an uncomfortable conflict, of which people as intelligent as Butler could not be unaware. The world had to be a benign and beautifully-calculated harmonious system, in order to prove God's goodness; while at the same time human life had to be in a serious mess, in order to prove our need of redemption. To make things still more complicated, the way the world now runs had to give us enough reason to believe in a moral Providence already at work within it; while yet there had to be large numbers of unrewarded virtuous acts and unpunished crimes left over, to make us look forward to a Future State in which God will finally balance the accounts!

However, eighteenth-century natural theology was in an even worse state than I have so far indicated. For the official natural philosophy, since the days of Robert Boyle and Isaac Newton, had been mechanistic and indeed atomistic. Maybe it was possible along Cartesian lines to lift the human mind out of it, but at any rate the world of physical bodies must be rigorously deterministic. In which case there could be no moral Providence discernibly at work in it. Newton's laws of motion would not hold universally if the world-process were subject to tinkering, so all the design of the world had to be put back and located in a stupendous primal computation of the initial position and velocity of each single atom at the first instant when the world was created. If the initial calculation were correct, then in due course the atoms must all run together to form human, animal and plant bodies. This has indeed happened; so the Creator must be very wise and powerful. And his universe must be deterministic.

Most writers were scarcely capable of tackling these difficulties. They contented themselves with trading on the fact that the available principles of scientific explanation – mechanism, atomism – were not sufficient to account for living organisms. From John Ray's *Wisdom of God* (1691) to the *Bridgewater Treatises* of

1833–40 the argument did not change at all, while the difficulties were mounting.

The eighteenth-century style of natural theology was vulnerable, above all, because of its extreme realism, both scientific and religious. God was proposed as an empirical hypothesis to account for the adaptation of nature to man, of organisms to their environment, and so on. But if God was merely a scientific hypothesis, then he was wide open to scientific refutation – as duly happened.

That point is obvious enough: less obvious is the scientific realism of eighteenth-century thought. If an argument from Design to God is to be valid and to reach a true conclusion, then we must be in possession of good and sure knowledge of the basic world-design. Nowadays, when scientific theory changes very rapidly, we are unlikely to make such a presumptuous claim; but in those days it was supposed that Newton had once and for all unveiled the con-stitutively-true theory of the world's structure. Nevertheless, even allowing for the relative stability of scientific theory in that period, people were being very bold in supposing that they were equipped to make trustworthy judgments about the wisdom and the benevolence of the plan behind the cosmos.

The old natural theology was also vulnerable in its ethical optimism. Being entirely committed to the classical episteme, it believed that the goodness of God could be inferred from the facts of nature because it was so convinced that Nature was benign, stable and harmonious. This optimism was not unchallenged even in its own heyday: Voltaire's protest in *Candide*, and Samuel Johnson's long indictment in his *Review of A Free Enquiry* (*Literary Magazine*, 1757) are both well known, and the challenge of T. R. Malthus (of whom more later) was even more powerful. But so strong is the influence of an episteme over one's judgment that William Paley continued to defend the popular optimistic natural theology even after he had read Malthus and had been convinced by his argument.

In retrospect this is astonishing. Malthus seems to a modern reader to force upon us a view of nature scarcely more cheerful than Schopenhauer's: the way the whole system of things is set up entails that every living thing can survive only by struggling successfully to get more than its share of the insufficient resources. How could Paley take in all this, and still give us the shrimps dancing on the sand and the rest of his rhetoric about animal happiness?[7] Evidently there is rather more to ideas of nature, natural morality and natural theology than we have yet acknowledged.

It is necessary at this point to put out of one's head any supposition that one already knows what nature is. All conceptions of nature are social creations, and have a social function.[8] We have to discover what that function is.

Begin, then, with classical antiquity, and with someone who encountered the diversity of cults in different cities and different lands and was thereby tempted to religious scepticism. Talk of natural theology and natural religion would have the function of reassuring such a person that there is a common and universal religious substrate beneath the local variegation. Here, the natural is the universal matrix that reassuringly underlies the locally varied forms of social life.

In the second place, insofar as the truths of natural theology were thought to be demonstrable, the natural becomes not merely the universal but also the metaphysical, the necessarily true, the foundational and, almost, the indisputable.

Now we aproach an ethical sense of the natural. Everywhere the natural is that to which we must resign ourselves. It represents the fixed, that which we cannot expect ever to be able to change. Thus the duty of respect for parents and seniors is natural, whereas homosexuality and incest are unnatural; and above all many, many things are natural (or unnatural) to women. Indeed, the reason why nature is a woman is that historically the appeal to nature has been used more than anything else to keep women in their place and to urge them to be content with it. It is allegedly 'natural' for woman to be pliant and docile, to be subject to man, to have a maternal instinct, to be more monogamous than men are, to suffer pain in childbirth, to be more emotionally unstable than men, to stay at home and look after the children – and so on, and on.

Thus nature appears to be a device that society uses in order to head off discontent. To portray something as being natural is to suggest that it just has to be the way it is and must be accepted as part of the permanently-given order of things. So society associates with nature all those clauses in its moral constitution which it is determined shall remain entrenched. For the natural is simply that which cannot usefully be questioned: it is the (supposedly) ineluctable.

However, the appeal to nature can be overpressed and can fail. The period when people most frequently wheeled out all the arguments about what is and is not natural for women was precisely the period when modern feminism was getting under way. People were beginning to make ironical remarks about the wonderful way in which nature always seems to step forward in the conservative interest, the interest of the patriarchs and the status quo, the interest of the haves against the have-nots. In fact arguments from nature eventually look ridiculous. They are so bad. They make nature herself seem like an ideological tool, a fiction. Those who use the arguments from nature seem themselves to be more than a little desperate, as if they know that they are losing.

That is what was happening in the eighteenth century to natural religion and natural theology. Far from being the strongest kind of arguments, arguments from nature are the weakest; last-ditch attempts to portray as immutable things that are in reality about to change very rapidly.

In saying all this, we are ready to continue the argument and to allow that the geologists and biologists were themselves developing a new conception of nature tailored to meet the requirements of an expanding and competitive industrial society. Yes indeed, and here we come full circle and return to the Vatican and Karl Marx, who were after all not wholly wrong to see in darwinism a mirror of the political economy of the society that had produced it. Yes, nature always mirrors society. But notice also that the new vision of nature that developed in the nineteenth century marks the end of the possibility of equating the natural with the morally fixed and unalterable, and prepares the way for the modern recognition that nature is in continual change because society is so. Every account of nature is a social product, and as society changes, nature must perforce change with it.

3

Time

The Earth has been rapidly growing older and older. In the mid-seventeenth century it was less than 6,000 years old (Ussher); but by the mid-eighteenth it was 74,000 years (Buffon), by the mid-nineteenth 24 million years (Kelvin) and by the mid-twentieth century its age had reached 4.6 billion years.

The human race has also been getting older, but at nothing like the same rate. Although the human evolutionary lineage is now traced back for many millions of years, fully modern Man, *H. sapiens sapiens* first appeared scarcely 50,000 years ago.

Finally, the Universe is currently believed to be about three times as old as the Earth.

Today, we are quite accustomed to looking up at the stars or at an ancient landscape and thinking how ephemeral we are compared with them. Yet that same thought horrified the young Tennyson, for it is not so very long ago that most people saw the Earth, the Universe and Man as being coeval.

Not only have our time-perspectives lengthened greatly, but the quality of time has altered. The change took place between 1687, when Newton first introduced his uniform, mathematical, linear conception of time, and 1884, when Greenwich Mean Time was established as the first recognized common world clock.

Before the Enlightenment, pre-modern time was something very different from our mathematical clock-time. Imaginatively and subjectively, time was an allegorical figure, Death's cousin and herald. With his hourglass he was a *memento mori*, reminding us of our finitude, of the uncertainty of life and the certainty of death and judgment. Because people lacked clear ideas of probability, and of planning for and insuring against future contingencies, they did not see any lengthy calibrated vistas ahead of them. They sensed only that the Last Things impended, and that the issue of life was in God's hands alone.

So far as society and its institutions were concerned, time was an erosive force like the sea. The world and everything in it had begun as people do, fresh, young and pure; but time means change, and change means decay. By a gradual attrition everything corrupts and shrivels, wears down and withers. Nothing is as good as it was.

The theological picture was more cheerful. The will of God gave time its direction and its stages. In fulfilling his purpose step by step, God moved the world through a series of great dispensations as he implemented his Plan of Salvation.

The important consequence is this: although European man always possessed a certain amount of secular knowledge of the past, his ideas about the future were until quite recently almost solely theological and derived from Revelation. Until the actuaries, planners and forecasters came along, attitudes to the future were almost purely religious.

Our modern experience of time is very different. Uniform, linear and religiously-featureless clock-time, no doubt because of the demands of machinery, communications and timetables, has come to dominate life to the point where we all wear watches and clock-time is the very form and frame of our experience. Kant's doctrine of the ideality of time as 'the form of inner sense' is perhaps a sign that the new uniform and mathematical sort of time had already become constitutive of the inner life of Westerners. People have come to view their own lives as planned temporal projects. They talk of what they are going to do with their lives and of where they hope to have got to by the time they are forty, of what they hope to become and of how they hope to be remembered. These are new lines of talk.

Nor should we assume that this new sense of time is quite secular and post-religious. On the contrary, the irreversible slipping-away of life, tick-tock, tick-tock, provokes in many a sense of bondage to time, and so produces a passionate desire for escape, for ecstasy and for transcendence. But there has been one change; for in Christian culture the longing for redemption traditionally took the form of an

Advent hope, a yearning to see the arrival of a new theological dispensation – the kingdom of God, the return of Christ. But the predominance of clock-time and the corresponding weakness of dispensationalism today means that the longing for redemption now commonly takes instead a more mystical and even Oriental form. We seek escape from the tyranny of the clock over consciousness.

However, modern time does not differ from pre-modern time solely in being mathematical rather than theological. It also differs in being creative.

Typical pioneers whose names are often cited at this point are Vico, Kant and Herder. Giambattista Vico (1688–1744) in his *Scienza Nova* (1725) is said to have pioneered the idea of historical development, at least in the sphere of Gentile history. (Biblical history was given a special status.) Vico is said to have grasped the ideas that a people's history passes through a series of distinct stages, and that each historical period is a coherent totality with no anachronisms.

It may be that Vico's originality has been over-stressed: certainly there is an obvious paradox in the claim that he was far ahead of his time in understanding that one cannot truly be ahead of one's time.[9] However, there is no doubt of the general point that during the eighteenth century people did become aware of the distinctiveness of an historical period and of the orderly, sequential character of historical development. In the same period Immanuel Kant (1724–1804), as we have already seen, produced a theory of cosmic evolution. Kant was the first to see God's creation of the world not as a single finished act but as an extended temporal process in which the law of gravitation, acting over long periods, forms galaxies, solar systems and the like. Finally, idealist nature-philosophy, beginning with J. G. Herder (1744–1803), amalgamated cosmological and historical ideas of development and introduced the idea that the whole of reality in its every aspect is an unfolding process.

In view of all this it is not surprising that the new historical sciences of geology and biology, as they developed, were regarded by many as being merely particular applications of the great master-idea of the age, the idea of development, of progress through struggle.

Furthermore, the discovery of time's creative hand had an important influence on the idea of causation. In the older world-view causality was something like the transmission of being and power down the line from greater to lesser. 'Cause' meant something like metaphysical ground, cause of being, or (metaphorically) 'father'.

In the newer world-view, however, the causal relation is less metaphysical. It is more like pattern-in-the-process, but with an important new feature; for whether we think in terms of mechanist determinism, or merely in terms of David Hume's regular successions, we have to face the puzzling fact that somehow the ordinary operation of causal laws results in progressive development.

This was a serious problem, for Newton had fixed in people's heads the idea that the operation of the laws of nature keeps the cosmos stable; and somehow it seems intuitively true to us that there cannot be radical innovation in a deterministic universe. In the days of Charles Lyell and Charles Darwin people were very conscious of the difficulty. No reintroduction of vitalism was acceptable to them. The main tradition of hard-headed science hesitated to become historical until it was satisfied that the ideas of universal mechanism and progressive development could be reconciled.

Both Kant and Buffon must have been aware of the problem, for they both evidently tried to meet it. The law of cooling in Buffon's theory of the Earth's history and the law of gravity in Kant's theory of the cosmos operate unchanged over long periods, and yet are able to produce sequences of complex effects as they do so. Could there be a similar mechanism-for-progress in biology?

4

The Making of the Earth

Originally, no doubt, every people believed that their own land was the best place, made for them and with everything just right, and that their own way of life was the best way of life. We may say that this fundamental confidence in the worth of one's own world is the most elementary form of religious faith. Where it is present, people can and will endure almost anything without complaint. The outstanding case is that of the Inuit, or Eskimos: they lived at the limits of endurance, in what for the rest of mankind would be intolerably harsh conditions, but their intense love for their forbidding territories and their way of life gave them great *joie de vivre*. By contrast, when that confidence is lacking we hear nothing but complaints: people feel alienated from the physical world and become highly conscious of the problem of evil.

Something of this primal sense of the goodness of our world and of our life was still around in the middle of the eighteenth century, communicated to people through the book of Genesis, and it influenced geologists as much as anyone else. Geology was always largely a practical science, concerned with things like mining and metal-working, drainage and building. Much of it is simply descriptive and classificatory. So in 1750 most geologists had little difficulty in combining their professional work as mineral surveyors, drainage engineers or whatever with a view of the created world that still owed much to Genesis, and with a time-scale that dated the creation of the world about 4000 BC.

Some anomalies, however, had already been noticed. In the seventeenth century Robert Hooke and a few others had already noticed the stratification of rocks, and had begun to learn to read the signs of long-term geological change: this river must have cut the gorge through which it runs; that hill with marine fossils in it must have been reared up from the seabed; in this silted-up delta sedimentary rocks are surely being laid down. Hooke had also noticed that many fossils are of strange creatures not now to be found. This was disturbing because in traditional thought the world is a *plenum*; every species that there ought to be exists throughout the world's history. If even one species had become extinct then the world was now deficient or flawed for ever, a very unpleasant thought.

None of this, however, could break people out of the established biblical time-scale. It was all very well to say that a chalkhill must have taken an immense period to lay down, but that was an ineffectual and platitudinous remark until some well-founded theories and numbers could be produced to pit against the formidably precise numbers given by Archbishop Ussher and others. Besides, the very idea of a scientifically reconstructible history of nature, history without personal agents, history prior to there being any observers or written records, was so novel as to be barely conceivable.

One way to get a grip on the problem was to speculate on what might be accomplished by a single force acting over a long period. As we have seen, at the large-scale level, Kant invoked the law of gravity and Buffon the law of cooling in this way. In geology something similar happened, one school wishing to ascribe all significant geological change to the action of water, and another to the action of fire. It was as if the theories of the Ionian philosophers – Thales and Heraclitus, perhaps – were being revived.

The Neptunists flourished first in Germany, and then in Scotland. A. G. Werner (1749–1817) was the greatest of them. He recognized and classified various strata and fossils, and noted the regular superimposition of strata, one above another. He argued that all the rock strata had first been formed by sedimentation, their rearing up and deformation by the action of volcanoes being a secondary and relatively recent phenomenon.[10]

By contrast, the best-known Vulcanists were French. J. E. Guettard (1715–1786) is said to have found clusters of hexagonal basalt columns in the French *Massif Central*. From his Italian observations of them he had already deduced that such formations were of volcanic origin. He was thus led to recognize the presence of long-extinct volcanoes in the *Massif*, and consequently the role of volcanoes in mountain-building. And to Vulcanists like Guettard it seemed obvious that sedimentation must be a secondary process, for it simply cannot occur unless relatively higher ground already exists and is being eroded, as sediments from it are carried down and deposited at lower levels. So the volcano, we must assume, is the prime builder of the landscape.

When Neptunist theories were taken up in Scotland by figures like Richard Kirwan and Robert Jameson, the claim that the action of water was the chief principle of geological change became entangled with the religious question of the Genesis Flood. Orthodoxy then demanded that Diluvialism, as it was now called, be defended a good deal more vehemently than was reasonable or prudent.

For, after all, there were obvious problems with Diluvialism. Certainly it supplied the biblicists with a gratifyingly enormous universal Deluge, but sedimentation is an extremely slow process which must in any case lead us to break out of the Genesis time-scale. And where had all the water gone? Furthermore, the Vulcanists clearly had a point when they said that water is a leveller. It erodes down mountains that already exist, but it cannot rear them up.

So James Hutton (1726–1797), in his *Theory of the Earth* (1795), attempted a synthesis. He was not a progressionist at all. Rather, he was a traditional Newtonian balance-of-forces man, and one who invoked the argument from design. In Hutton's theory, therefore, the Earth is maintained in an approximately constant and habitable state by the combined action of several different geological forces, including both the upbuilding work of fire and the levelling work of water, going on together over a very long period.

The unlucky Hutton found himself at the centre of a very fierce controversy, out of which the next two schools of thought emerged. His critics felt they were losing their biblical Flood, and that Hutton's theory laid so much emphasis on the uniform long-term action of natural causes that it left no place for a personal Creator to show his hand. The result was the Catastrophism of men like Georges Cuvier (1769–1832) in France, and William Buckland (1784–1856) and Adam Sedgwick (1785–1873) in England.

The Catastrophists were reacting against Hutton's uniformitarianism. They could foresee it turning into a purely secular geology, and they dreaded the coming of an age in which the physical world would be fully explained by positive science, and God's action would be restricted to the sphere of human psychology, or the inner life. A God who acts *only* through secondary causes and the laws of nature, and never directly, is virtually an absentee from the world. So the Catastrophists were holding out for a personal interventionist God. His great acts of destruction and recreation had established each major geological epoch upon the ruins of its predecessor. Matched roughly with the Days of Creation in Genesis and with the signs of progression in the fossil record, Catastrophism could be, and was made to appear, both biblical and progressionist. As evidence in its own favour it could point to the apparent discontinuities between one era and the next which appear in the very fact that strata are distinguishable. Even to this day there is still a trace of Catastrophism in our own popular belief that 'the extinction of the dinosaurs' is an event and a problem that calls for a special explanation.

However, there was something very odd about the Catastrophists' theology. In the Bible catastrophic interventions of God have a moral purpose, as when God smites the wicked city of Sodom. I am able to recognize an earthquake as an 'act of God' insofar as I first know myself to deserve punishment and then recognize this event as being what I deserve. Moral desert and coincident event have to fit together in a morally appropriate way. But in the case of Georges Cuvier's numerous prehistoric catastrophes the necessary reference to the human and moral realm is lacking. For whose benefit was God putting on the firework displays? Who was being admonished? As religious events, the catastrophes were absurd and could not do the job for which they were intended, of reassuring us about God's moral providence and personal rule.

The Catastrophists were bound to lose the argument because their religious 'literalism' was religiously preposterous, and also because Hutton's idea of several different natural causal principles working over an extended period was much more versatile and scientifically fruitful.

For the new historical sciences of nature are, as we now see more clearly, hermeneutical. The aim was to learn how to look at a geological feature and read its story. Hutton's plurality of causal factors made the hermeneutics imaginatively interesting. It taught us to inspect the feature and work out for ourselves just what mix of agencies – volcano, earthquake, glacier, river, rain and frost, waves and so forth – must have shaped it.

So the Huttonian line of enquiry was bound to win because it was more intellectually interesting, and it did so when Charles Lyell (1797–1875) had his *Principles of Geology* published (Volume 1, 1830). Lyell was able to reconcile mechanism and progression, and he argued that the discontinuities between strata of which the Catastrophists had made so much did not matter, because the gaps found in one place are in fact filled in another.

But the victory of Lyell, and the further triumph of the same principles in Darwin, was something like a fatal blow for interventionist versions of belief in God as Creator and Governor of the physical world. Furthermore, to a thinker like the young Tennyson it was apparent, well before Darwin published the *Origin of Species*, that the new vision of the world-process threatened to make animal and man alike into mere transient products of nature, called into existence for a while and then discarded. Within our souls, he says in 'In Memoriam' (sections LIV and LV), is something that speaks of God and of immortality, but nature says the opposite:

> Are God and Nature then at strife,
>   That Nature lends such evil dreams?
>   So careful of the type she seems,
> So careless of the single life. . . .
>
> 'So careful of the type?' but no.
>   From scarped cliff and quarried stone
>   She cries, 'A thousand types are gone:
> I care for nothing, all shall go. . . .'

And so, the poet asks, shall 'Man, her last work,'

> Who trusted God was love indeed,
>   And love Creation's final law –
>   Though Nature red in tooth and claw
> With ravine, shriek'd against his creed –
>
> Who loved, who suffer'd countless ills,
>   Who battled for the True, the Just,
>   Be blown about the desert dust,
> Or seal'd within the iron hills?

Tennyson's answer is considerably less good than his question, for he eventually takes refuge in a decidedly vapid liberal theology. There are other and perhaps nobler answers: the ethical heroism of

Albert Schweitzer, the turn to the East and in particular to Buddhism, Jung's discovery of the imperishable world of the psyche, and so on. As for Tennyson's question, it is as urgent today as it was when he asked it, one hundred and fifty years ago. And perhaps Nietzsche, more than anyone else, has seen what kind of answer can alone be fully satisfactory; for he saw that we must somehow find our way back to the primal affirmation of our world and our life with which this chapter began.

5

Malthus

T. R. Malthus (1766–1834) was a mathematics Fellow at Jesus College, Cambridge when in 1798 he produced an anonymous pamphlet called *An Essay on the Principle of Population, As it affects the Future Improvement of Society, with Remarks on the Speculations of Mr Godwin, M. Condorcet and other Writers.*[11] Its success encouraged him to undertake extensive research, for which he travelled abroad, and the second edition of 1803 is a substantial book, and maybe the first major scientific work about human society.

As the title suggests, Malthus was arguing against those who believed that the human lot on this earth could be steadily bettered until some kind of perfection was reached. Perhaps unfairly, he has thus generally been seen as a pessimist and a conservative. The basic argument runs as follows: Animals and plants, as everyone acknowledges, have great powers of increase which are held in check by the laws of nature and by environmental constraints. We human beings, it would appear, are in the same position. For in newly-colonized territories which offer almost boundless scope for expansion, such as the United States, human populations have in fact proved capable of doubling in every twenty-five-year generation. Since 'the passion between the sexes' is presumably nearly constant in its effects, we may safely generalize and claim that human populations, when unchecked, will double every twenty-five years.

Yet this potentiality for geometrical population growth cannot for long be matched by a corresponding rate of increase in the means of subsistence. The most that we can expect is that the food-supply may be increased in an arithmetical ratio. It follows — and, as Malthus believed, this conclusion expresses a law of nature — that in every long-populated country there must be constantly-operating checks on the growth of population.

What are these checks? Malthus' accounts of them differ slightly, but the essential point is that the limitation of the population may be either voluntary or involuntary. Either we control the birth-rate, or 'positive' checks such as starvation, disease and war must come into operation. For the situation is as it is with an equilibrium of forces in Newtonian mechanics: the power of multiplication must be counterbalanced by the sum of the various checks, and if one check is weakened there must be a corresponding increase among the others.

There is much that is wrong with Malthus' argument, and especially with his assumption that fertility is more or less constant. It now seems well established that fertility declines as a country becomes richer, even though many more children could easily be fed; and also that fertility may decline alarmingly among a people whose morale is low. Malthus did not encounter any country like modern West Germany. He was also too pessimistic about the possibilities for food production. Setting aside more exotic ideas, the productivity of the land can be increased very rapidly by better plant-breeding, fertilizers and pest-control, and still more by the simple expedient of eating grain directly and converting less of it into meat and dairy products.

If these objections are question-begging, then let us take a simpler one. In the modern USA the population is approximately stable, but do we have any evidence that people are therefore unhappy because they are in some way being prevented from having as many children as they would wish?

It seems then that Malthus gave his argument too brash an appearance of mathematical rigour, and modelled his population theory too closely on Newtonian ideas. Still, he was right to sense that in future society would need to have a population policy: even China, for so long sharply hostile on political grounds, now concedes that point to him. And he was also a portent for the future in his attempt to bring at least one important area of our lives under a mechanistic scientific theory, and in his insistence that we are inescapably subject to the laws of nature.

Both Darwin and Wallace attested Malthus' influence on their own independent formulations of the theory of evolution by natural selection. Here we have a classic case of ideas passing from physics to social science, and from social science to biology – and all the time with strong, though contested, political overtones.[12] It is a case that clearly suggests that our various branches of knowledge are not and can never be wholly autonomous and independent of each other. They are better thought of as being different aspects or functions of a single cultural totality.

So far, so familiar; but there is something more yet. In chapters XVIII and XIX of his first edition Malthus ends by assessing the consequences of his doctrines for natural theology. His framework is traditional: he is asking how his own harsh view of life can be compatible with belief in the good Providence of God, and he is answering in terms of the argument from design and a theory of life as a state of probation. Yet although the framework is traditional, Malthus says some novel things within it. He does so because his account of the human condition so much emphasizes our need for foresight, prudence and self-discipline if we are to survive. God, it appears, has so designed the world that we must develop and use our wits if we are to survive; so that Malthus becomes, I think, the very first psychological evolutionist.

Malthus was of course no kind of biological evolutionist. He was a Newtonian, working within the classical episteme. For him, forces so operate as to produce quilibrium, and he has no suggestion that the struggle for existence might bring about biological change. But in the psychological realm he goes further. God has designed the world as a school of virtue, and Malthus (in his rather schoolmasterly way) evidently sees developing and stretching one's intelligence as a moral duty.

So Malthus is led 'to consider the world and this life as the mighty process of God, not for the trial, but for the creation and formation of mind, a process necessary to awaken inert, chaotic matter into spirit. . .'. He classifies 'the great awakeners of the mind' under three main headings. There are, first, the wants of the body: our environment does not naturally provide us with sufficient food, clothing and shelter, and we must use our wits and our hands to get them. Secondly, there is the constancy of the laws of nature and the great advantage to be gained by discovering them. Thirdly, the sex-drive itself, and the very fact that our power of multiplication always tends to run ahead of the resources presently available, gives us a strong and constant stimulus to bring more land under cultivation, and so to expand our economy.

Malthus is of course working within the classical episteme and with a moralistic view of the mind. But a little modernization of his language can make him seem startlingly up to date, for he is saying that the human mind has been generated by the pressure on us of our simple biological needs, and that it reflects and responds to natural regularities. By the end of the century, after the completion of the shift to the new episteme and after Darwin, it would become common for people to see nature as a theatre of conflict, the mind as a natural product, and our knowledge as being a complex kit of skills for survival. In Malthus there are already present some seeds that would germinate when the general climate changed; but no doubt neither he nor his contemporaries could see in his text what we with our hindsight now see.

There is more in Malthus yet. We suggested earlier that the most primal kind of religious faith is the ability to affirm the goodness and meaningfulness of our own way of life and our own world-view. We have also suggested that the typical eighteenth-century idea of nature, together with the argument from design, may be seen as still standing in that ancient tradition. No doubt, as many have said, there was in this an element of cosmic Toryism:[13] 'Whatever is, is right.' But there was also a genuinely religious attempt to claim that the whole scheme of things makes sense, is good, and is fitted to us as we are to it. As a religious man of his time Malthus stands in that tradition, and is attempting to continue it in the face of an emerging harsher vision of nature. Although life surrounds us with inexorable limitations, although unalloyed happiness is not possible, and although we are seemingly embedded in and products of nature, yet we can still say a religious 'Yes' to life.

Malthus' followers included religious optimists and religious pessimists. William Paley (1743–1805) in his *Natural Theology* (1802) was a highly optimistic liberal Anglican follower of Malthus. Though they often sound rather quaint, his observations often have more than a grain of sense in them. Thus he says of venomous animals that they have a right to live, that they also have a place in the scheme of things and need their own means to defend themselves and to kill their prey; and in any case, they live chiefly in deserts where they do us little harm. So we should not think them evil. On 'superfecundity', or the question of animals' excessive powers of multiplication, he notes that it is in the animal's own interest, especially if it is a small and vulnerable creature, that it should be able after a setback to restore its numbers rapidly; but that in that case there must also eventually be checks on its power of multiplication. We human beings, Paley adds, are part of this whole scheme of things and subject to its laws; and it teaches us prudence and virtue.

Although Paley's idiom can seem a little comical to modern ears, the way a modern biologist thinks of the living world that is his subject-matter is perhaps not so very different, whereas another Malthusian, the Scottish Calvinist Thomas Chalmers (1780–1847), who founded the Free Kirk, may be less congenial. In the Bridgewater Treatise of 1833, on *The Adaptation of External Nature to the Moral and Intellectual Constitution of Man*, he criticized Paley for taking too benign a view of God, and as a result treating evil in a superficial manner. For Chalmers, society is part of nature, and God has constituted the natural and social worlds on analogous lines, so as to make our life a moral discipline, a school of virtue.

What then is virtue? Chalmers sees both nature and society as being so made as to require of us a moral policy of competitive *laissez-faire* individualism. The school of virtue is the rational pursuit of survival, of self-interest, and of the increase of one's own property and pleasure.

Chalmers was an ultra-conservative Presbyterian minister. Once again we see that there is an intimate relationship between a person's view of nature, and his political and religious views. It is as if a small group of basically ethical decisions and postulates underlie all three. But at what point and in what way we make these ultimate choices, why different people make them differently, and why the consensus on them slowly shifts over time – all this remains largely unknown.

6

Life, Before Darwin

The belief that life is a supernatural mystery, not fully explicable in physical terms, persisted till very recently. Often such beliefs are not very fully articulated, but in this particular case the main lines are fairly clear. As a rule, where there is any sudden movement in the environment, it is a sign of the presence of a living thing. Life is movement, the movement of heart and blood and breath, and the power to initiate movement. So what distinguishes a living body from a corpse is the presence in it of a principle of life and motion, and this is called soul. Furthermore, it seems that purely physical bodies may transmit motion, but cannot initiate it in the way that animate beings can. All motions must sooner or later, then, be traced back to soul and, in Plato's words, 'soul is the oldest of all things': the Prime Mover must be soulish.

In this way there was a connection between the ideas of life, soul, movement and God, which implied that God is living and that all life comes from God. Hence the idea that life is a supernatural mystery, and the theological sensitivity of biology as a subject. Darwin himself, in the *Origin of Species*, has the Creator breathing life into the first organic forms.

It is often said that a major obstacle to the reception of darwinism was the idea of the fixity of species. Because the terms genus and species are Aristotelian, and it seems to be a general requirement of Aristotle's philosophy that things be classifiable into natural kinds, we assume that the fixity of species was a long-held traditional idea.

But this cannot quite be so, for several reasons. Since antiquity people had believed in the existence – or at least the biological possibility – of large numbers of monsters of decidedly mixed parentage. Secondly, they also believed in the idea of the Great Chain of Being, and the chain was continuous, each member being merely infinitesimally different from its neighbour, which suggests that there are not objectively distinct natural kinds.[14] Classification is conventional rather than natural. It cuts up what in reality is a continuum.

So it may be more exact to say that the fixity of species was not so much an ancient idea as rather a recent achievement of classical thinking, in the work of great taxonomists like Linnaeus. Even then, matters are far from clear. The first modern-type definition of a species, by John Ray (who had plant species in mind), saw it as a kin-group. A species is a class of organisms which in principle might all be plotted on one big family-tree. But then, what about all the plant hybrids, varieties and sports? They surely make it impossible to be over-dogmatic about the immutability of species and the supposedly unbridgeable gulf of infertility between species. Yet now we are on the brink of the idea of evolution, for if we agree that a species is a descent-group, with varieties branching off it and connections by hybridization with other species, then we have imagined an evolutionary tree in miniature. The relation between the wild Sea Kale and the various cultivated brassicas in our vegetable plots is of just this kind.

Thus even those like Cuvier who by repute were keenest on the fixity of species could not afford to be too rigid about it. The evidence prompted one to think as much of evolution as of fixed kinds. And the same was true in other areas of biology. The facts about the irregular geographical distribution of living things, the succession of the rocks, and the succession and progression of the fossils embedded in the rocks were all pretty well understood by 1809, when Lamarck published the first evolutionary tree.

The same can be said of the evidence of comparative anatomy. Comparative anatomists – being, it seems, a conservative group, like surgeons in the medical profession – were prominent against Darwin. Yet the evidence of their own subject surely told for him rather than against him. On the catastrophist view God started afresh when he made the birds, and started yet again when he made the mammals; so why in that case did he create modified reptile

skeletons for each of them? For that matter, why begin from and then
severely distort the standard mammalian forelimb, if you want to
create the whale's flipper and the bat's wing? And why create
vestigial organs? Almost everything in comparative anatomy points
to evolution rather than to special creation.

The evidence was all in place by 1810 or soon afterwards, and yet
the triumph of evolution was delayed. The main reason is fairly
clear: those who did put forward evolutionary ideas were rather
woolly vitalists like Herder and Lamarck. Such writers could not
convince a man like Charles Lyell, who was an orthodox Newtonian
mechanist and uniformitarian. He disliked even the idea of progression, because it was associated with catastrophism and vitalism; so
that even in the 1830s, in his *Principles of Geology*, he still would not
admit progression in the fossil record.

Again, surely, the problem was one of episteme. Lyell was
attached to the older ways of thinking. He liked a stable mechanistic
physical world with man in a distinct and privileged position to
observe it, and he preferred this world-view on both scientific and
religious grounds. By the same token, he did not care for the new
Romantic and pantheist merging of man into an unfolding natural
process. He would be persuaded only when the shift of episteme had
gone far enough to make a mechanist progressionism plausible. At
this point we might compare Marx's dialectical materialism with
Darwin's, and we notice that Darwin's theory is more soulless than
Marx's. It allows a larger role for chance, and strictly speaking has
no guarantee of progress at all. Though Darwin to some extent
glossed over the austerity of his own theory, many of his contemporaries grasped the point. Perhaps, like Lyell himself, they accepted
Darwinism in the Protestant tradition of taking a rather 'low' view of
the physical world, while secretly reserving a special status for their
own minds and consciences. We are ourselves probably the same to
this day, for while it is possible – though not altogether easy – to
learn to look at animals and plants and see them as simply natural
products of chance and time, variation and selection, it is far more
difficult consistently to think of one's own thinking as mere natural
process and as a product of evolution. There are horrors ahead here
with which few of us have yet grappled.

One further aspect of biology before Darwin deserves a mention.
The subject of heredity is of universal interest to human beings, with
its bearing on their own family relationships and on the breeding of

their domesticated animals and plants. Yet neither his immediate predecessors nor Darwin himself had any theories of value about it. Around 1750, P. L. M. de Maupertuis had arrived at a substantially correct theory, but his work was disregarded, as was also the work of Darwin's contemporary, Gregor Mendel.

Why this gap? Patriarchy appears to be to blame. Since classical antiquity the predominant assumption had been that the father alone determines the character of the offspring. The woman was simply the field in which he sowed his seed. The preformationist theory popular in the eighteenth century, according to which the next generation sit like tiny crouching babies in the heads of the male spermatozoa, merely continued the old error – and since those little homunculi had the third generation ready-made in their loins, and so on *ad infinitum*, evolution was also ruled out.

But during the early nineteenth century, coinciding with the first stirrings of feminism, the contribution of the female parent came gradually to be recognized. In the old days it had been supposed that the male implants his seed directly into the wall of the uterus, but in 1827 the embryologist von Baer discovered the ovum of the female mammal. The new and extraordinary realization slowly diffused itself that a woman is an active and creative sexual being in her own right. People call Darwin a patriarch, but in fact in the *Descent of Man* he has the new outlook, for he was the first to show the biological importance of sexual selection by the female in shaping the future of the species.

There is, therefore, a close but as-yet-unexplored link between genetics and feminism.

7

Darwin and Our View of Life

At some time around the mid-nineteenth century, or a little after, scientific naturalism became the dominant world-view in our culture. It has since spread around the globe, though there are still some sharp reactions against it here and there. It is the doctrine that the only way we can understand and explain any event in nature is to see it as an instance of a recurrent pattern of similar events in nature. The physical sciences in particular hope to define these regularities mathematically. In the humanities things are rather different, but the human sphere is also part of nature, and within it an action is intelligible insofar as it is 'typical', the sort of thing experience has led us to expect. Naturalism is immanentist, for it presumes that events in nature can be explained only in terms of other events in nature. In this light, talk of what is supernatural or transcends nature seems no longer to make sense. We do not see how it could be well-founded.

The triumph of naturalism in our culture, even if it is by no means complete, is a very important and remarkable event; and it was brought about, as much as anything, by the argument of Darwin's *Origin of Species*. The key ideas came to Darwin in the great creative period in London, 1837–39, during which he wrote the *Notebooks*. From these materials he fashioned a *Sketch* of the theory in 1842, and the booklength *Essay* in 1844. In the 1850s he embarked on a very large version, working on it for several years until abruptly compelled by the news of Wallace's work to prepare the version that was published in 1859.

The central argument of the *Origin of Species* is analogical. As by the breeder's artificial selection from among the variations that occur in a domesticated species the stock is eventually transformed, so we must presume that the struggle for existence in nature brings about, by natural selection, the gradual transmutation of species. Alongside this central argument Darwin lays out a wide-ranging survey of the evidence of the geological record, the geographical distribution of living things, the facts of taxonomy, embryology, and rudimentary and vestigial organs. The aim is to persuade us that the evolutionary theory makes better sense of this vast field of facts than does any other theory.

From the first Darwin knew that there were real and serious objections. The whole argument was circumstantial; evolutionary change had not yet been observed. The weakness of the genetic theory available to Darwin made him unable to say how, starting from a single individual, a favourable variation could spread through a whole population rather than merely be diluted away. Nor was it altogether clear how a population managed to split into two mutually infertile groups, as must happen whenever an extra species is added to the whole number. And Darwin failed to recognize the possible importance of sports, or mutations.

This was not the end of his difficulties. The terrestrial time-scale allowed by Lord Kelvin's calculations seemed much too short, the fossil record was thin at some key points, and there was no knowledge of the past movements of the continents to help explain many details of geographical distribution.

So Darwin had many problems. Yet in spite of them, and despite the fact that evolution can still to this day seem an astonishing notion, he won quite quickly. No doubt the whole culture, almost against its will, was already prepared for the idea. Apart from the episteme-shift we have mentioned, we should consider also that in Darwin's lifetime the church was losing overall control of the culture, autonomous scientific professions were developing, and the very word 'science' was coming to be used in the sense of natural science, as if it were now becoming agreed that natural science was the exemplary case of genuine knowledge. Still more important, the universities were taking on their modern role as the major centres for criticizing and increasing the vast new bodies of secular knowledge. Darwin's book was the Genesis, and his theory the unifying creation-myth, for the new culture: that is why evolutionary and functionalist ways of thinking were taken from biology and applied to so many other subjects, and why in the eyes of so many in the churches darwinism and unbelief were synonymous. Darwin had supplied the new age with its most important single myth.

He had done this not only because the theory itself was so very wide-ranging, historical, broadly progressive and naturalistic, but also because it seemed to incorporate man himself, and presumably all his works, so thoroughly into nature. Seventeenth-century science had ended with a split world-view: there was the mechanical universe, and there was the world of the minds or spirits who are the observers of the mechanical universe. But now in the modern period Darwin seemed to open up the possibility of a thoroughly unified world-view.

However, there were some difficulties. An evolutionary account of man suggests that our knowledge is a mere set of survival-skills. Yet when we formulate evolutionary theory and judge it true we act as if we are ourselves entitled to be scientific realists with a 'strong' theory of knowledge. Is this compatible with the picture of us and of our capacities that is given *within* the theory? Darwin himself said that he thought that the lowly origin and the practical character of our cognitive powers disqualified us from discovering the answers to the great metaphysical questions of life. But in that case it might also disqualify us from being confident scientific realists. Some of the American pragmatists were to find themselves in this difficulty. Keen darwinians, they argued for a pragmatist theory of knowledge. But then it was pointed out to them that one could not argue from the dogmatic truth of darwinism to the pragmatic character of all our knowledge without absurdity. William James was already vividly aware of the difficulty and defined his own version of pragmatism with some subtlety in order to meet it.[15] But the task of explaining and justifying human knowledge within the context of a consistently naturalistic world-view is still not completed.

The problem of spirituality, of the religious life within the new world-view, is even more difficult. We will return to it, but it is necessary to give it a first airing at this point.

Darwin himself was, or rather, professed himself in the *Origin of Species* to be, optimistic. It was reasonable to believe that the living world had a very long period ahead of it, and that this would be a period of continual all-round improvement.

However, there was no basis for this optimism. The truth was rather that Darwin had shown in the most brutal way that the natural world, the process that has brought us into being, is non-moral. We do not fulfil any larger purpose, there is no moral world-order, and our existence is utterly gratuitous. Our natures have been formed by millions of years of ruthless competition, so that it is scarcely likely that they can be changed radically. We are trapped.

Thoughts like these lead in something like a Schopenhauerian direction, suggesting a mood common in the first post-darwinian generation. Thomas Hardy is its finest representative. The way life is perceived is coloured by an implicit contrast with something else that has only recently been lost. So there is a sense of exile from a lost paradise, of settled melancholy, of a brooding watchful conscious-ness, and of bitter complaint about the cruelty and meaninglessness of life, all the more deeply felt for there being nobody left to address it to. Since the novel can no longer display and celebrate the moral world-order, it has to take a symbolist and aesthetic turn, making the human tragedy endurable by transfiguring it artistically.

Thus described, Hardy's world-view is not so far from that of the young Nietzsche. It prompts the thought that we are quite wrong in supposing science and industry to be so dominant in modern culture that art has little place. The truth is the opposite: for over a century now our view of life has been so bleak that we have had to tell ourselves stories constantly to keep our spirits up. Most people in one way or another consume many times more fiction (through radio, TV, cinema, magazines, drama, novels, etc.) than ever people did before the nineteenth century. We twitter about the weakness and the poor quality of 'high art', forgetting that art has now perforce become democratic on the very largest scale. It is needed for survival. This is the century of art. The fact that so much of it has to be predictable and optimistic entertainment, with assured cosiness and happy endings, only shows the more poignantly how desperate people have become.

However, Schopenhauerian nostalgia and resignation are only a first-generation response to darwinism. The next stage is to cast them off. As the singer tells us at the end of the opera *Cunning Little Vixen*, life in the forest is renewed every spring forever, so why should man alone be melancholy? There is nothing else but life's brief and furious self-affirmation, so philosophy must turn towards a biological naturalism that says 'Yes' to life.

This may take various forms: in Nietzsche the life-impulse is heroic individualism; in Renoir and Picasso there is quite explicit fusing of the sex-drive with artistic creativity; in Lawrence a fierce insistence on a kind of biological integrity in the emotional life, and so on.

In such figures we glimpse the real ethical and religious outcome of darwinian naturalism. It sets us within nature and requires us to see ourselves as products of nature; of the earth, and returning to it. The ethical outlook that corresponds to this is biological naturalism, while the traditional religious demand for purity of heart and inner integrity now takes the form of a demand that our highest ideals shall not deny or do violence to, but rather be an integral expression of, our biological being. We have to unify our various roles, as expressions of biological life, as human and social beings, and as the pursuers of spiritual ideals. The neglected Scottish philosopher John Macmurray was a good exponent of these themes.[16]

However, we have not yet raised the question of darwinism and belief in God.

8

Darwinism and God

During the nineteenth century natural theology developed through five distinct stages.

At first, in a figure like William Paley, a world-view more than a century old was to be found still surviving intact. Natural theology and natural philosophy were barely distinguished from each other. The design argument displayed God as the wise and benevolent Author of Nature. Creation had taken place all at once, by special divine act, with occasional subsequent miraculous interventions.

Stage two is the period of belief in Epochs of Nature, or in Catastrophism. The most moderate form, Hutton's, imagined an initial supernatural creation followed thereafter under the Providence of God by uniform geological epochs. The thoroughgoing catastrophist doctrine taught by Cuvier, by contrast, declared that there has been a whole series of supernatural acts of destruction and recreation extended over a long period of time.

At the third stage, the world's creation ceases to be supernatural and God is seen as working only through natural laws. Thus the world takes shape by the slow and uniform action of secondary causes, again over an extended period. A few special creative interventions by God within the process are however retained. Charles Lyell is the greatest exponent of this view.

Next comes full uniformitarianism with no remaining special interventions, whether in geology, biology or even in anthropology (i.e., so as to create the human soul). When no special interventions are left, the conception of God becomes deist or agnostic. Darwin and Huxley were not quite atheists, nor even quite pure agnostics, for Darwin has a faint trace of a First Cause and Huxley has a sense of an invisible opponent. They are perhaps best described as minimal deists, in the manner of David Hume's *Dialogues*.

Finally, at stage five there are the various forms of atheist materialism or positivism which deny outright the meaningfulness of the metaphysical questions that had still troubled Darwin. With this denial, no place is left for metaphysics as a superscience. Only at this last stage is natural theology completely eliminated – though there are, of course, many who will say that it is still too early to write the obituary of metaphysics.

In what ways, then, might acceptance of darwinism be combined with a realist belief in God?[17] Asa Gray, Darwin's distinguished American correspondent, took what we have called a 'stage three' view, as being no doubt closest to the traditional orthodoxy: a supernatural first creation and thereafter the uniform operation of secondary causes, with occasional special interventions. However, Gray was aware that 'the uniform operation of secondary causes' was not the same thing as God's general Providence. Providence, after all, was supposed to be moral and purposive, which the operation of natural selection was most certainly not. Darwin's account of the harsh mechanism of evolutionary change leaves no room for any moral influence on the evolutionary process once it is in motion. So Gray thought that God had preplanned and calculated the whole system, and then set it rolling in the foreknowledge that it would eventually produce you and me without requiring any further guidance or interference.

Darwin wondered if this meant that we were to suppose that God had preplanned all the degenerate organisms, the parasites, and the bizarre varieties elicited by human breeders. This was not an especially novel comment, because mainstream theism, or much of it, had of course been broadly predestinarian since early times. Naturally the God of classical theism, being all-powerful and all-knowing, eternally foreordains every detail of the world process. That had long been believed, and Darwin had not discovered any fresh difficulty in believing it – except that his new and clearer insight into the character of the process that has brought us into being has raised questions about the morality of the world that God has chosen for himself to have. To put it bluntly, was this *really* the best that God could do?

Post-malthusian religious conservatives – as we saw in the case of Chalmers – could reply that although the process God has chosen is admittedly harsh in detail, nevertheless the overall outcome of it is good and the world works very well as a place of moral discipline. But what kind of morality? To a modern reader Chalmers appears to advocate ruthless *laissez-faire* individualism in both nature and society, and to be claiming that it makes for a good, and even a Christian, character. That is odd: but even odder is the implied claim that God has set up a godless system in which it is every man for himself and the devil take the hindmost – and has done so in order to bring us thereby to himself. Nothing could bring out more clearly the sceptical strain in high Calvinism.

Non-calvinist writers were unlikely to produce anything so aggressive as Chalmers' teaching. Rather, during the thirty years following the publication of the *Origin of Species* they developed a new liberal theology which emphasized the ideas of development and progressive revelation.

This liberal theology had the concurrent advantage of also offering a solution to another burning issue of the time, biblical criticism. It was an old idea that the Bible is a microcosm, the world epitomized in a text. Looked at in the new historical way, the Bible revealed a process of development from the primitive deity of the early Israelite tribesmen to the exalted vision of the divine love at the summit of the New Testament revelation. There has been a progressive revelation of God through the unfolding story of the long struggle of the Jewish people. In the Bible it appears that God's way is progress through conflict and suffering – and perhaps Darwin is saying the same about nature? Even in this new era there is then perhaps still an analogy between revealed religion and the course of nature, of the kind that Bishop Butler taught us to perceive.

So reasoned some of the first generation of young post-darwinian Christians. They included G. J. Romanes (1848–1894), a scientist and layman of Caius College, Cambridge, Aubrey Moore (1848–1890), an Oxford man and the author of *Science and the Faith* (1889), and the country clergyman and idealist philosopher J. R. Illingworth (1848–1915). The best-known figure of the group was to be Charles Gore (1853–1932), with whom the full Idealist hierarchy arrives: the world-process, he declares, successively attains the levels of Matter, Life, Mind and Spirit, and God reveals himself more completely as each new level is reached.[18]

These writers and others like them were the creators of a tradition
of liberal theology that is still alive. We shall find it worthwhile to
examine in some detail the way it reshaped the system of Christian
doctrine in response to darwinism. I shall describe what might be
called an 'ideal type' of it, somewhere between Gore, F. R. Tennant
and John Hick.

Throughout we must bear in mind that liberal theology still
cherishes the old ambition to provide a grand controlling myth for
the culture as a whole. It understands Christianity in cosmological
terms, therefore, attempting to synthesize scientific and religious
world-views in a single epic narrative. This in turn implies that
scientific and religious beliefs alike are being understood in 'realist'
ways.

The revision of the main heads of Christian doctrine then goes as
follows: In the traditional doctrinal scheme, as found in St Augustine
and others, there was a once-for-all perfect Creation of the world
from the top downwards (that is, God began by creating the angels),
a created order that is subsequently conserved by God's Providence.
In the liberal revision of this we are asked to think in terms of a
continuous creation of the world from below upwards, along
broadly uniformitarian and non-interventionist lines. The world-
process moves towards a completion and perfection of the world
that lies still in the future.

Moral evil and suffering in the world had been seen in the past as a
secondary corruption that had entered creation after the first human,
or perhaps angelic, sin. For the liberals, though, the world begins
imperfect and pre-moral, as babies do. Value is realized only
gradually, through struggle and suffering. This has to be so, for God
chose the world to be a vale of soul-making, and a mature and free
moral personality can be forged in no other way.

The older theology looked back to Eden as an age of primal
perfection, when human beings had lived in a state of original
innocence and righteousness and enjoyed a natural communion with
God. Even as late as the twentieth century there were still some
learned writers who defended the idea of 'primitive monotheism' –
the claim that belief in one God was the earliest form of religion. But
the liberals preferred evolutionary ideas. The race grows from
childhood to adulthood in the same way as the individual, so it was
natural that religion, like everything else, should develop from
primitive beginnings – totemism, or animism perhaps – to a final

fulfilment that is yet to come. We should think in terms not of the descent but of the ascent of man; of his progress rather than his degradation.

The doctrines of the Fall and original sin therefore come in for considerable revision. Orthodoxy insisted that the Fall was an historical event, a sin committed by a primal couple from whom all subsequent human beings are descended: a quasi-biological transmission, as of an hereditary disease, was envisaged. Liberal theology was compelled to revise this, for there was no way in which we could have historical evidence about the very first human beings, so long before the invention of writing, and no way in which the human race could be traced back to a single couple. The minimum unit on which the forces that bring about evolution can work is the gene-pool of an entire population. There was no evidence for a prehistoric Golden Age of mankind, and, what is more, the notion of original sin as a kind of hereditary disease, and as a mass punishment in perpetuity, was absurd.

So instead the liberals said that human beings have always fallen short of what they might be. Sin may be seen, perhaps, as a residue of our animal background, coupled with the finitude which makes selfishness seem almost natural to us. Alternatively it might be said that sin is a social, rather than a quasi-biological, taint: we are born into a sinful society and corrupted by it from the first.

Other writers suggest that our first emergence out of the primal unity into individual self-consciousness brings about in each of us a sense of alienation. We feel 'alone and afraid, / in a world I never made'; a condition to be overcome by the development and pursuit of moral and spiritual values.

In the classical theology God brought about our redemption by a once-for-all and final revelation of himself, as recorded in the Old and New Testaments of the Bible, and above all by his incarnation and his atonement with us in Jesus Christ. The liberals, as we have seen already, wished to generalize the idea of revelation and to make it progressive, and were strongly devoted to the historical Jesus. It might be thought, then, that they would simply retain the traditional centrality of Christ as the focus of all human history. However, this was not easy to do. Given their strong commitment to the idea of historical development, they could scarcely avoid the thought that in time the whole world-view of the New Testament must become unintelligibly remote and outdated. Indeed, some said that this had

already happened, so might not Jesus himself eventually be super-
seded by the passage of time?

To this there were two possible lines of reply. Liberal protestants
such as Harnack and Albert Schweitzer regarded the core of Jesus'
ethical teaching as eternal, and as continuing to stand even though
everything else about him slips into the past. The difficulty with this
is that Jesus' ethical teaching then becomes *a priori*, timeless and
with no necessary connection with any historical teacher. We may,
and in the end we probably must, keep the teaching and discard the
teacher.

This point of view is Kantian; it is Protestant ethical idealism. The
alternative to it is more Hegelian and Catholic. We say that the
totality of what Christ is and has been and is yet to be to men is still
developing, and its final meaning is not yet known. What began with
the incarnation must ultimately extend to the whole human race and
to the end of time. The source may be remote by now, but for that
very reason the river flows all the more mightily.

The next doctrinal revision need be mentioned only briefly: in
traditional theology Christ's redeeming work was understood as a
victory over evil powers, as a cosmic sacrifice offered on our behalf,
or even as a vicarious suffering of the punishment due to us for our
sins. The liberals, influenced by nineteenth-century humanitarianism, sought a more ethical interpretation of the atonement. Christ
saves us by the moral attractiveness of his example, the sheer power
of the ideal of self-giving love.

Finally, the older Christianity had been strongly dualistic in the
way it contrasted this life and the life to come, the City of Man and
the City of God, the saved and the lost, the church and the world, and
so on. But liberal theology was always universalist in temper. It
thought less about the church than about the destiny of the human
race as a whole, seeing the kingdom of God as the goal not merely of
ecclesiastical history but of all history. It rarely mentioned Hell, and
because its chief interest was in the human future on this Earth it
often had little to say about life after death.

The liberal theology therefore represented a considerable revision
of Christian doctrine. It had conceded so much to the progressive
and historicist spirit of the age, and it so far played down anything
dualistic or miraculous, that it might be described unkindly as an
updated and historicized form of Deism. There were in particular
two disastrous failures.

In the first place, in spite of its claims, the liberal theology had not really reckoned with darwinism at all. The darwinian view of nature is, strictly speaking, non-moral and non-progressive. We are chance products of an amoral process that gives no sign of caring a jot for us. There is no objective reason to claim for ourselves any special status in the cosmos, and the cosmos is not going anywhere. It is merely in very slow decay which will eventually leave nothing but radiation. No version of the liberal theology known to me has even begun to grapple with these propositions.

The second failure of liberal theology was equally serious. Attempting to reconcile science and religion, it interpreted religious beliefs in an objectified and realist manner, and interwove them with scientific (or supposedly scientific) beliefs. In a quasi-scientific way, it placed itself firmly in the objective sphere, and left out of account the bearing of religious beliefs upon the subjectivity of the single individual. Almost all of liberal theology lacks Kierkegaard's kind of inwardness and religious seriousness. He would object that it has lost the Christian categories, that particular set of determinations of the spiritual life which simply *is* Christianity, and he would surely be right to say so.

The liberal theology, then, was neither truthful enough nor religious enough. Its two failures were connected. In the seventeenth century Pascal, facing up to the eternal silence of the infinite spaces, was forced back upon Christ, the human realm and the heart. Similarly, in the twentieth century it may be necessary first to recognize the godlessness of the objective world, and therefore the disjunction between the domains of religion and science, if we are to learn to interpret religious ideas correctly.

9

The Radical Alternative

Like both Paley and Darwin, the liberal theologians were science-and-religion monists.[19] By this ugly phrase I mean that they all of them understood both scientific theories and religious beliefs in a realist way, as purporting to describe objective states of affairs. Science and religion were both producing maps of the same world. They were moving in the same territory, and were potential competitors in the same market; all of which meant that in principle they could either enter into conflict with each other, or alternatively (as by the liberals) be synthesized.

Given that after about 1860 science became the dominant knowledge-system in the culture, whereas religious belief had been so beforehand, it is not altogether surprising that the liberals should have acted as they did. They were attempting to transmit the old faith forward into the new world view. So they revised the old world view and interwove it with the new. But they seriously underestimated the gulf between the two, and the systems they produced did scant justice either to Christianity or to the truth of the human situation as it has come to be perceived. Interweaving scientific and religious ideas produces a kind of mythology or science fiction which is in fact both bad science and bad religion.

So we take the other path. We reject any attempt to synthesize scientific and religious beliefs and instead accept the autonomy of natural science within its own sphere. This in turn means that we accept the naturalistic outlook, not because it is currently taught as part of the conclusions of natural science but simply because naturalism is a presumption of science. However science develops, we can be sure that its outlook will remain naturalistic. None of this, of course, commits us to scientific realism, nor suggests that natural science does anything at all to answer the fundamental questions of life. We simply acknowledge that science is what it is, and is a distinctive way of construing the world.

Now we characterize the difference between the methods and provinces of science and religion. In natural science we learn the habit of bracketing-off or setting aside our own subjectivity, and seek understanding and control of nature as from the viewpoint of an ideal observer. Scientific language aims to be logically neutral and to define all terms and theories as precisely as possible, with the object of achieving unambiguous public communicability and testability. Scientific meanings and procedures are meant to be quite indifferent or neutral as between individual persons. Who you are does not matter.

By contrast, the religious attitude to life is intensely self-involving, committed and ethical. Its axiom is that the measure you get is the measure you have meted out; the way reality is for you depends upon just what you are and what you have put in. As the proverb says, we each make our own bed and must lie on it. There is thus an element of voluntarism in the religious view of life: the choices I make shape my destiny by helping to determine the way the world is going to be for me. The language of religion will therefore naturally be expressive: that is, my religious utterance expresses my feelings and intentions and is part of the religious activity by which I order my life and my world. Religious truth will be something that is appropriated by participation; that is, religious belief has to be enacted and tested in practice. It is a form of practical wisdom, true insofar as it proves reliable in my life. And finally, religious meanings will not have the same kind of neutral and public precision as scientific meanings. They will be more like aesthetic meanings; condensed, symbolic and multivocal. Indeed, one might define religion as an attempt to put into one's own life what a creative artist attempts to put into his work.

The religious is therefore the existential, or the subjective. Typical forms of religious discourse will be confession, testimony and preaching. The religious is that which pertains to the 'manner' of my own existence as an individual human person, and a religious communication to a person is typically one that requires him to examine and to change his form of selfhood and way of life.

Although in traditional society stories about the creation of the world and about the first human beings may be told to all in order to prescribe a standard world to live in and a standard form of personhood for everybody, the account I have just been giving implies that there is not in fact any absolute world-order, independent of what we are. Rather, what is called the world is largely (or wholly?) a shadow cast by human activities. To change our world we must begin by changing ourselves and our social relations, for 'reality' is a function of the values we choose to live by.

From this it is clear that religious doctrines are practical imperatives, or in Wittgenstein's phrase, 'rules of life dressed up in pictures'. They communicate our values.

It has been suggested that this amounts to saying that religion is to be demythologized into ethics and spirituality, that dogmatic theology must be translated into ascetical theology, that faith is only a way and not a theory. But this is misleading, for no translation or reduction is involved: there simply is not anything else that religion could ever possibly have been. We have not given up anything except the illusion that something else could coherently have been said. So we are not denying that religious beliefs are objectively true, in any sense that implies that they could have been something that in fact they are not. On the contrary, they do not lack anything that they could perhaps have had. They just are what they are.

The point here is fundamental. Before we first set about critical self-examination, our thinking was full of little knots called 'literal truth', 'objective existence' and the like. When we examined these ideas closely, they dissolved away and at first we felt a sense of loss. But then we realized that there was not in fact anything that we had lost. We were not without anything that could possibly be restored to us.

This happened to us most recently with 'realism'. We asked ourselves what could be meant by realism, and answered that the meaning of realism must somehow be given in the arguments that are urged in its favour. Those arguments are, after all, intended to differentiate it from its competitors, which supposedly lack its advantages. But we could find no argument in support of realism which clearly indicated what it was, by defining some condition that it fulfilled, some test that it passed, or some advantage that it possessed that differentiated it from its competitors and showed what it was that they were not. We could not find anything that realism was, and so it faded away. We saw that it is one of those things in which, as they say, you 'have faith' – in the popular but questionable sense in which you are instinctively inclined at first to be sure that there is something *there*, although this turns out to be the sort of instinctive conviction of objectivity that dissolves and disappears when we look carefully. But once this pre-rational 'faith' (so-called) in realism is gone and I am adjusted to the loss, why then, I no longer miss it, and I do not consider myself to be excluded from anything. I have simply become a little clearer in the head, and that is all there is to say. Arguments between realism and anti-realism do not after all mean much, for if the former is a non-thing, so is also the latter.

So it is with the transition to the modern attitude to religious belief. We prove able to make the adjustment. As a matter of fact, for centuries and even for millennia the number of invisible spirit-beings, magical powers and energies, occult harmonies and corres-pondences around us has been getting less and less. The universe has been getting thinner and more abstract. Each stage of loss at first seems a disaster, but we get used to it as we see that only an unthing was lost. Once the universe seemed a home, but then with the rise of modern science we became chronic aliens. There is no other consciousness out there at all. But then we acknowledge that the former sense of being at home in the world was after all only an illusion. What have we lost? – nothing. And now we see that in any case we ourselves make all our representations: our world-view is, in a strong sense, our own. Our astronomy is just as much a man-made artefact as our own dwellings are. Obviously our astronomy is not our homeliest artefact, but if it feels too cold to us then we are entirely at liberty to set it aside for a while and take up instead something homelier such as religion or fiction. All of which is to say that the romantic, old-fashioned Heidegger-and-Sartre talk about man not being at home in the world is dated now, for there is no meaning in the suggestion that we are *objectively* either at home in the world or not. If you feel alienated, turn to something homelier. That is all there is, all there can be, to say.

What then of the reconciliation, or whatever it is, between science and religion? Is our radical point of view so *laissez-faire*, is our thinking so little constrained by any objective reality (if such an expression can be permitted), that religious belief and scientific theories are quite independent of each other?

Not quite, for we are still going to come back in the end to the unity and coherence, both of people's lives and of the world-view embodied in their ordinary language and activities. Scientific theories are often rather abstract and specialized, but when they are tested experimentally they are tested against the view of the world presupposed in ordinary life, and in ordinary laboratories. There is of course still a place for experimental testing on our account, and scientific theories in their own way have to be tied back to our common life in our common world. And in religion there is a still stronger commitment to coherence. For religion is precisely about the unity of my life, and of our lives together, and about the value and meaning with which we are to invest our lives. The unity and simplicity of God is a symbolic expression of the required unity of the religious life, and as our society is now completely reliant on scientific knowledge in its day to day functioning, we have to reconcile the scientific and the religious attitudes.

That is the difference between us and the liberals. Unaware of language, not even aware of the nature of human knowledge, they attempted an objective reconciliation of scientific and religious 'facts', an enterprise that now seems rather quaint. The one thing modern about them was that their revision of religious meanings was carried out in so free a way as to constitute a tacit admission that all such meanings are human constructs – though they did not say so, of course. But we are more modest. We seek only to live an examined and religiously-unified life. Religion is after all an attempt to live a life that is not haunted by a chronic sense of dissatisfaction, absurdity, futility and shame at one's own existence. And to live a life that is religiously-unified in a science-based culture will require a subjective reconciliation or harmonization of our scientific and our religious attitudes and activities. Hence our emphasis, in Chapter 7 above, on working out the naturalistic ethical implications of darwinism and relating them to religious ethics. A study of, for example, the ethics of sex would be an excellent way of working out the implications of biology for religious belief without becoming involved again in the mistakes of the past.

10

Eternal Life

The point is not commented upon very often nowadays, but at the time it seemed to many people that the most obvious and most traumatic corollary of darwinism was the end of belief in an afterlife. The new historicism suggested that human existence was a transient episode, and a minor one at that, in the vast ongoing cosmic process; and the new naturalism made it very difficult to imagine what a supernatural mode of human existence could possibly be like. Consider for example the shift in our view of women since Darwin, and all the new things that have arrived for them: far better physical health, competitive sport, sunbathing, the cult of the body and more awareness of female sexuality, increasing legal and social equality and economic activity, and so forth. The shift is towards a more activist and biological picture of human nature, and it is not surprising that during the same period ordinary people have found it becoming increasingly difficult to represent life after death to themselves in any imaginatively convincing way.

At the same time, as we watch closely the ways in which people speak about death we notice that large sections of the language and the idioms have always taken it for granted that death is simply the cessation of life. Thus we know that we pass this way only once, and must eventually come to the end of our days. We may hope to be remembered, and aim to leave our corner of the world a slightly better place than we found it. When our time comes we will breathe our last, the doctor will pronounce life extinct, and nothing will be left of us but our corpses, our testamentary dispositions and anything else on which we may have left some slight impress of ourselves. Death should not be seen as being simple extinction, for to die is to become a corpse, and a corpse is still spoken of in (qualified) personal terms. However, a corpse is something that needs to be disposed of, and a hint that the living are not always anxious to know that the dead are still around can be found in the practice, known among various peoples, of binding the limbs of the dead to prevent them from coming back to trouble the living. Our feelings may sometimes be more mixed than we care to acknowledge.

That upon death we cease to be active living persons and become instead corpses is so blindingly obvious that one may well ask how people could ever have thought otherwise. And why were the Victorians so shocked at the loss of such a manifest illusion?

In the same vein, I note a recent writer criticizing sharply what he calls 'the religious denial of death' – and thereby inadvertently giving us a clue. For he is clearly wrong. Religion did not deny death: on the contrary, the admonition *Memento mori* was an important part of religious rhetoric. Worldly people would often accuse Christianity, not of denying death, but rather of being unduly and morbidly preoccupied with it. To do justice to the religious attitude to death we need to take account not just of the rich expressive imagery of an afterlife, but also of the normal religious insistence on transience and the need to live a recollected life in which each day is as if our last. The aim was not to deny the finality of death, but rather to live from moment to moment in the power of the eternal, and so to achieve the synthesis of time and eternity that the believer calls 'eternal life'.

One can see here how easily talk about life after death may become openly non-factual. Religious thought may thus learn to become adult in the same way as philosophy has already done, the essence of maturation being that we give up pretending that norms are facts. We let norms be just norms, without any longer wishing to reify them or to invent a special world for them to inhabit. So the believer's eternal life is not a life after death, nor a life lived with one eye on an unseen world, but simply life lived by an eternal standard. What does that mean? It means that we habitually demand of ourselves inner truthfulness, singleness of purpose in the pursuit of virtue, spontaneous emotional integrity, and the spiritual poise that comes with the right mix of commitment and non-attachment. To live like that, to live really well, is to have eternal life.

So it is rather easy to demythologize traditional beliefs about life after death, and in these historically-minded days it is hard to avoid doing so. To the historian, eschatological symbols are very varied and unsystematic, even within a single religious tradition. They function as promises and admonitions, and reflect current social concerns. The rhetoric of death and the Last Things is always a social construction, and takes exceedingly diverse forms around the world and in different periods. He aims to understand it, and to see what job it does. And that is all he has to say: for him, neither belief nor disbelief in such things is any longer an appropriate attitude to take.

Again, the Victorians had plenty of notice that all this was coming. They were already debating during the 1850s, just before *The Origin of Species*, F. D. Maurice's proposition that 'eternal life' and 'eternal death' are primarily phrases that describe states of soul, rather than cosmic places.[20] Why the trauma?

The reason is that much more was at stake than the status of talk about Heaven and Hell, and the destiny of the individual. In the past, religious belief had been sustained by the idea that although things were admittedly pretty dark just at the moment, there had already been a time in the past and there would again be a time in the future when all was plain. But now, however, critical history had destroyed the belief in an original perfection, and the loss of belief in life after death was destroying the hope of an eschatological perfection of the world. People had put up with their present darkness because they cherished a blessed memory and a glorious hope. Now they lost both, and the present darkness became, it seemed, the one and only known condition of religious existence. The nineteenth-century crisis of faith was a dawning suspicion that there never has been and there never will be significantly more of God around than there is just now. The answers to the ultimate questions of life will never be one whit more clear to us than they are now. Human nature never has been and may never be noticeably better than it is just now. The problem of evil, the horrific random cruelty and injustice of life, may always be fully as bad as it is at just this moment. The fundamental conditions of human existence always have been, and always will be, very much as they are now. Pictures of a Primitive Golden Age and of a Final Golden Age are just myths. They are not factual: rather, as is always the case with myths, they help us to see our true situation more clearly by inviting us to contrast it with an imagined other way that things might perhaps have been. Understood in this way, as consciousness-raising devices, myths are indeed very helpful. But to nineteenth-century pessimism this was small consolation for the loss of the old conviction that the human condition had really been naturally perfect in the past, and would become supernaturally perfect in the future.

What seemed to remain was a symbolist view of religious beliefs. They are consciousness-raisers, they dramatize for us the questions of our existence, and they embody and communicate our values. They are vitally important to us, for they give us the standards we are to live by – but they are not factual. There is not any literal meaning in the idea that one might outlive one's own life; the very notion is a manifest absurdity. But, still more important, the nineteenth century cultural revolution destroyed a whole conception of religion that one might call the spirituality of deferred satisfaction.[21] The notion of life after death was just one aspect of a whole metaphysics of alienation which portrayed the believer's present situation as being one of exile from his proper home. The way things are with us now was supposed to be neither intellectually satisfactory, nor morally satisfactory, nor religiously satisfactory. We do not have sight, but are confined to the outer darkness of mere faith. The real world in which we ought to be living is elsewhere, Yonder, on the far side of death. So to be a religious person was to be radically dissatisfied with one's present conditions of existence and to yearn passionately after a heavenly Jerusalem, a true world elsewhere. The more alienated you felt in this world, the more sincerely and admirably religious you were – and it is this entire way of thinking that has now been destroyed. After Darwin, religion must reconcile itself to this earth.

There is a possible reply, and it runs as follows: We can think about ourselves in two different ways, or from two different points of view. If we think about ourselves from an objective and scientific point of view, then indeed we are just physical organisms, bound by natural law; and from such a point of view it is plain that darwinism has integrated us into the animal kingdom and left us with no more reason to believe in our own life after death than in that of any other animal.

However, that objective scientific point of view is to a philosopher naive and question-begging. Instead we should take several steps back to a standpoint within our own experience. From this subjective point of view each of us is to himself a series of experiences, mental states and intentions more or less loosely or tightly bound together, and the whole metaphysics of the body and the bodily world is as yet an open question. And why should not this succession of experiences – just *go on*? To an empiricist the tie to the body may not seem necessary. To see why, imagine that you are dreaming, and quite oblivious of the current state of your body. Is it not conceivable that your house might be blown up and your body destroyed – and yet your dream simply continue? From an empiricist point of view our experiences are philosophically primary, and do not have to be seen as dependent upon states of the body. For it is the body that is logically secondary. All talk about bodies is constructed from experiences, and not vice versa: so that the objective cessation of my bodily being is not necessarily the termination of my subjective experience.

Along these lines, then, many empiricists have been ready to treat life after death as an open question. There may be a dearth of positive evidence for it; but equally, there are no conclusive arguments against it.

This empiricist tendency to belief in life after death – 'Why should not the chain of experiences just . . . *go on*?' – will only be seriously undermined if it can be demonstrated that our subjective experience is just as deeply bound by biological laws and categories as is my objective and bodily existence. If I am not merely bodily close kin to my dog, but also psychologically of one stuff with him, then my chances of making myself out to be a special case are very much reduced. It is to psychology that we therefore now turn, and to the interesting question of how far we already have or will one day have a natural science of the mind.

PART II

THE MIRROR OF THE SOUL

I

Science and the Mind

Psychology has been called a subject with a long past in story, drama and religious confession, but only a short history.[1] As a science it has been in existence for little more than a century. Before then it was difficult, and seems to have required uncommon talent, for human beings to look in a cool and objective way at themselves.

In a few areas the attempt to look scientifically at things human goes back a long way: censuses, the medical examination of the body and the dissection of corpses. But all of these were formerly regarded as impious. Society and man were defined in theological terms: they not only belonged to God but were themselves considered to be sacred mysteries, created and maintained by divine power. They were too holy to be examined with a profane eye. Thus in the Bible David sins by taking a census: population statistics are God's affair, not the king's. And as with the body politic, so it was also with the body of the individual; because its secrets belonged to God, various taboos and restrictions were laid upon nakedness, corpses, the medical examination of the body, and the preservation and display of human remains.

Attitudes to nakedness and the genitals are often instructive. In Genesis the genitals are covered because as the source of life they are sacred and belong to God. One may swear an oath by them. In India the cosmos is often drawn in the shape of a human body, the spine corresponding to the *axis mundi* and the vertebrae to the layered heavens and hells. In meditation such ideas are transferred back to one's own body, as the focus of the meditator's concentration ascends his own spine and mounts to the top of his own head. The human body thus comes to be seen as a microcosmos, an hierarchically-ordered sacred system whose baser parts should be veiled.

More generally, right up to the present century most people did not – and perhaps they still do not – look directly at themselves but rather assessed themselves in terms of their relation to ethical and religious norms and standards. This self-examination vis-à-vis a moral norm is entirely different from the scientific type of self-examination. Detailed explanations are not really called for. It was sufficient to recognize oneself as being a sinner, or more specifically as a glutton, a miser or whatever, and then to proceed directly to the appropriate corrective action. The aim of self-examination was practical and ethical. You sought to grasp which of the allegorical characters you were playing in life's great morality play.

Since human nature seems to be a cultural creation, we must suppose that in those days life really was a morality play in which everybody acted out the part of a stock character. Only when the culture had become more complex and differentiated would society create more diverse inner lives for us. In the later Middle Ages the prevailing ethical and religious norms were so dominant over life that not only people but even animals, the fox, the goose, the sheep and the rest of them, were conscripted into becoming emblems of moral qualities. While that was so, people could scarcely have the attitudes to animals, to nature and to the biological element within their own make-up that became possible after Darwin.

In at least a weak sense, the idea that the mind is a cultural creation is unavoidable. For we speak of the mind always in metaphors, and since all the metaphors in terms of which we understand ourselves are inevitably drawn from the society in which we are set, what we can be to ourselves is determined by our social circumstances. A century ago computer models of the mind were impossible; today they are obligatory. It follows that our thinking about ourselves is datable, period thinking. And, naturally enough, as the Western scientific tradition developed it supplied successive new metaphors for the slowly developing sciences of man to use.

Briefly, then, the beginning of the study of anatomy in Western Europe (Mondino, thirteenth century) coincides with the acknowledgment by Christian thought of a sphere within which human reason may operate autonomously. In the Renaissance the study of anatomy (Vesalius, Fabricius) is associated with humanism in art. The mechanist tradition in science was applied straightaway to the body – including the brain – by Descartes and, even more boldly, to the mind by Hobbes. The most influential for psychology of the great philosophers of the period, was, however, John Locke, who quite consciously models the mental world on the physical. As there are atoms, compounds and laws of motion in the external world, so in the world of the mind there are simple and complex ideas, and laws of the association of ideas. Locke thus gave rise to a tradition of Associationist Psychology that reigned for almost as long as the Newtonian physical science whose mental counterpart it was.

This Associationist Psychology had two features worth remarking. It somehow combined, without explaining how it did so, the 'bittiness' of atomism with a full Cartesian confidence in the complete and perspicuous presence of the self to itself in self-consciousness. Secondly, the picture of the mind as a system of simple and compound ideas moving around according to laws of association had some important implications. It was in effect deterministic. It identified, or at least confused, the laws of logic with the laws of psychology. And the models it relied upon might be called chemical, but they fell far short of being biological.

In the early nineteenth century, Hegel introduced the idea that the mind develops historically from lower to higher levels of consciousness, with the corollary that mentalities are different in different periods; and Schopenhauer became the first to break with the Cartesian idea of consciousness, teaching a more biological doctrine of the mind that in many ways anticipates Freud. However, the biological revolution proper arrived with Darwin's *Descent of Man* (1871) and *The Expression of the Emotions* (1872), which revealed the possibility of an evolutionary, biology-based and scientific psychology.

If the mind is indeed an historical and evolutionary product, from what testimonies could we ever hope to construct its history? The task is not quite so impossible as it seems. If our embryology can give clues to the evolutionary history of our bodies, then by the same token the earliest development of children may give clues to the history of the human mind. Similarly, comparative zoological studies may give clues to psychological evolution as well as to biological evolution generally. Next, we may add historical and cross-cultural studies. Nor is this all, for Nietzsche in the 1880s had already suggested that dreams may give us insight into the most archaic regions of the mind.

Evidence is then available, and there is no reason to despair of the task. And if the mind has been built up layer by layer on a biological base, that basis presumably consists in the biological drives to food, self-preservation, sex and so forth. And we may suppose that culture is an immense system of signs and learned behaviours which utilizes the energy of these biological drives, eliciting it, transforming it and redirecting it.

However, when we thus begin to build up our account of the mind from below, some disturbing new questions arise. Traditional doctrine did not envisage the human soul as ever less than fully conscious and rational, but our brief sketch suggests that on the contrary self-consciousness is not essential to the mind at all. We could manage without it. It has been added secondarily; some say, less than three thousand years ago. But if so, then we have to ask what its function may be. Why did we develop it at all?

One of the earliest answers remains one of the best: Nietzsche argues that consciousness is social.[2] It exists to facilitate mutual co-operation and understanding within human groups. Its absence makes a difference, as when we notice the way that very small children in a playgroup can play oblivious of each other. But the consciousness that enables us to be curious about, to guess and even to feel the corresponding feelings of others may also have disadvantageous consequences for us, by making us suffer disabling feelings of guilt, anxiety and impotence. So Nietzsche, obsessively original as ever, became the first to suggest that self-consciousness may be pathological. Like the Homeric heroes, we might be better off without it.

A related insight, whose origin I do not know and cannot date, is as follows: consciousness can no longer be thought of as increasing in a uniform way like a light controlled by a dimmer switch that is being steadily turned up. It cannot be measured on a single scale, and I am no longer clear that we should speak of degrees of it at all. On the contrary, because self-consciousness is functional, and is relative to the current state of culture, the forms it takes can be as varied as cultural forms generally. And obviously it may develop the strangest blindspots, as gains in some areas are offset by losses in others (losses which are not disabling, because human beings do not need much consciousness, and there is no single area that *must* be brightly lit). Bruno Bauer, and maybe even Nietzsche, thought that the most lucid introspection was attained by those who were most perfectly disillusioned, whose minds were most sceptical and demythologized. But if so, what of Augustine?

Finally, the new biological approach to consciousness prepares us to accept that the unity of the mind is not metaphysical but merely organic, and a matter of degree. We need not go quite so far as the Buddha and David Hume, who thought that we are just a succession of experiences. The unity of my self is simply the unity of my life and my bodily history – from which it follows, by the way, that there is no point in talking about any disembodied or post-mortem self, abstracted from my life and my bodily history.

The psychology we shall be talking about in these chapters is, then, the modern, biology-based and post-darwinian psychology. But the word is a little older than that. It was first used in the sense of 'mental philosophy' by Christian Wolff in 1732, and by Hartley not long afterwards, in 1748. The adjective is said to have been invented by Coleridge. The first work of scientific psychology is probably Francis Galton's *Hereditary Genius* (1869), which marks the beginning of psychometrics. W. Wundt established the first laboratory of experimental psychology at Leipzig in 1879, but four years earlier William James had already taught the first academic course in the subject.

As for the psychology of religion, there was of course an immensely strong literary tradition in the nineteenth century: it is sufficient to name such great figures as Feuerbach, Kierkegaard, Dostoevsky and Nietzsche. But the scientific tradition was established by William James, to whom we turn next.

2

Healthy-Mindedness

William James (1842–1910) was born in New York, the eldest of five talented children.[3] Their father, Henry James senior, was a man of leisure and a writer. He was an undenominational Protestant who was influenced by Swedenborg, by the Transcendentalists and by the contemporary optimism which identified the realization of the American national ideal 'one out of many', *e pluribus unum*, with the coming of the Millennium.

The Jameses illustrate a kind of radicalism that comes readily to Americans, but only with difficulty to Europeans. Its philosophical expression is pragmatism. Unburdened by a medieval past or by a heritage of metaphysics, Americans are naturally anthropocentric in outlook. The past left behind, people had set themselves to build a new nation in a virgin land, and had succeeded. In such a context it is not surprising that at least some Americans have been much more ready than Europeans to see all aspects of culture, including religion, as products of human constructive activity, expressions of human nature.

In his celebrated book *The Varieties of Religious Experience* William James does make out a case for a supernatural reality with which religion is concerned. But the case made out is perfunctory by European standards, and the reader is much more impressed by the breezy confidence with which James throughout his book assumes that religion is just a natural and wholesome outgoing expressive human activity. Ludwig Wittgenstein, who was inclined to religious gloom and had laboriously fought his way backwards to anthropocentrism, found this aspect of James helpful; whereas to the Oxford metaphysician R. G. Collingwood it was detestable.

In 1861 James began to read chemistry at Harvard, switching two years later to comparative anatomy under the influence of Agassiz, and then again after another year to the School of Medicine. In 1865 he went on an expedition up the Amazon. It was at this time that his years of depression began: he took no part in the Civil War, and although he took his MD in 1869 he had no wish to practise medicine.

In the *Varieties* James included, suitably disguised, his own autobiographical account of his state of mind in his depression. It is to be found near the end of the lectures on 'The Sick Soul'. As with everything he wrote, it speaks for itself:[4]

Whilst in this state of philosophic pessimism and general depression of spirits about my prospects, I went one evening into a dressing-room in the twilight to procure some article that was there; when suddenly there fell upon me without any warning, just as if it came out of the darkness, a horrible fear of my own existence. Simultaneously there arose in my mind the image of an epileptic patient whom I had seen in the asylum, a black-haired youth with greenish skin, entirely idiotic, who used to sit all day on one of the benches, or rather shelves against the wall, with his knees drawn up against his chin, and the coarse gray undershirt, which was his only garment, drawn over them inclosing his entire figure. He sat there like a sort of sculptured Egyptian cat or Peruvian mummy, moving nothing but his black eyes and looking absolutely non-human. This image and my fear entered into a species of combination with each other. *That shape am I*, I felt, potentially. Nothing that I possess can defend me against that fate, if the hour for it should strike for me as it struck for him. There was such a horror of him, and such a perception of my own merely momentary discrepancy from him, that it was as if something hitherto solid within my breast gave way entirely, and I became a mass of quivering fear. After this the universe was changed for me altogether. I awoke morning after morning with a horrible dread at the pit of my stomach, and with a sense of the insecurity of life that I never knew before, and that I have never felt since.

In 1872 James obtained a junior post in physiology and in 1876 he taught the course already mentioned on physiological psychology. In 1878 he married, and four children followed. The happiness this brought cured him psychologically and liberated him to write, during the years 1878–90, *The Principles of Psychology*.

Although James' writing about psychology is well-grounded in biology and physiology, it contains little reference to experiments or to measurements. His chief interest lies in what might be called philosophical psychology, and his chief asset is his literary style. Two centuries earlier, John Locke had sought by introspection and descriptive reporting, his 'historical plain method', to set forth the life of the mind, and James was now doing something very similar, but with a modern outlook and with much superior equipment.

On the strength of his theory of the emotions James has been called a materialist, but in reality he was not attracted to any kind of reductionism and in particular was opposed to associationism. The mind was not to be constructed in the old mechanist way, from atomic constituents and laws for assembling them, but was rather to be seen as a living organism. It is with James that the new post-darwinian self enters psychology.

According to James, consciousness is a continuous living stream of experience. It includes the apprehension of relations and of wholes, as well as the atomic perceptions and ideas recognized by associationism; and it includes both transitive and intransitive states. Like the visual field it has a penumbra as well as a focus, for in addition to the clearly-defined thoughts that are most salient in our minds there is always an extensive but vaguer stream of semi-conscious material flowing past. As a beam of light may be directed to different areas on the surface of a river, so we have a good deal of freedom to direct our attention to this or that area of our experience.

There is a further respect in which consciousness is mutable and fluid: because the self is an organism it is continuously responding, changing and adjusting itself to stimuli from the environment. For James there is no permanent, and unchanging metaphysical Self or soul-substance. Indeed, why do people feel the need for one? Since the metaphor of a river, the stream of consciousness, recurs so often, let us pursue it. We have no difficulty in identifying the river Thames, even though we cannot dip into it and take out any particular thing that makes it uniquely the Thames and not some other river. Nor would the Thames have any stronger identity if we were to lay a continuous cable along it from its source to its mouth, or if we were to line it with concrete to prevent its banks from moving. So what can people be asking for, and why are they asking for it, when they ask for an extra being, a metaphysical soul, to function as the principle of identity? If the river Thames does not need such a thing, why should I need it?

James thinks that we neither possess nor need to possess some one thing that by being one and unchanging secures our continuing identity for us. However, we do indeed have a complex image of ourselves as continuing persons. It is partly physical, depending on the continuity of our bodies, our looks, our clothing, our homes and our familiar surroundings; partly social, depending on the roles we daily enact; and it is partly given us by the body of long and short-term projects on which we are at any time engaged. All these things, combining, give coherence and continuity to our lives, and therefore to our selves. But it is certainly possible for dissociation to occur within this complex whole, and in extreme cases it may produce a split personality. Less dramatically, the felt self may quite normally shift and change its location within the psyche just as the field of conscious attention may shift. James gives as an example the President who is 'a different man' when he is able to get away for a fishing holiday.

Against the background of this view of the self James has what is – again, by European standards – an amusing, original and very American conception of religion. Religion is simply a personal concern for one's own subjective well-being and goals. James makes his point by saying that science is to religion as menu to food. Science creates an objective diagram of the world from which individual subjectivity and its interests have been excluded, so that to someone trained in the scientific outlook religion cannot but appear as a relic of primitive animism and wishful thinking. Religion, however, is solider than science. It is 'the food', for religion is about the subjectively lived experience of life, its process, its self-affirmation and its destiny. So James declares roundly that religion is quite properly egoistical, or eudaemonistic. He disparages ascetics such as the Buddha and St John of the Cross, and at the end of the Varieties effectively identifies faith with the capacity to enjoy life:

It is a biological as well as a psychological condition, and
Tolstoy is absolutely accurate in classing faith among the forces *by
which men live*. The total absence of it, anhedonia, means
collapse.[5]
And James goes on to quote J. H. Leuba's pragmatist view of God:

> The truth of the matter can be put in this way: *God is not
> known, he is not understood; he is used* – sometimes as meat-
> purveyor, sometimes as moral-support, sometimes as friend,
> sometimes as an object of love. If he proves himself useful, the
> religious consciousness asks for no more than that. Does God
> really exist? How does he exist? What is he? are so many irrelevant
> questions. Not God but life, more life, a larger, richer, more
> satisfying life, is in the last analysis the end of religion. The love of
> life, at any and every level of development, is the religious
> impulse.[6]

In religion James is an unapologetic pluralist and consumerist: the
religion a person stands by 'must be the one that is best for him, even
though there were better individuals, and their religion better than
his'. Religion is in the end little concerned with 'logic truth' or with
seeking 'to solve the intellectual mystery of the world': its concern is
with 'lived-truth', with what sustains our self-affirmation and makes
us victorious in life. We have the right to believe, and the right to
choose the form of belief that will do us most good. And James is so
insistent that religion is about our personal happiness that he will not
allow it to be identified with morality. Their moods are opposite,
ethics leading us to strenuous self-criticism and pursuit of what
ought to be, whereas religion typically cultivates a mood of passive,
relaxed satisfaction with things as they are. Morality is all very well,
but the bow must be unstrung from time to time, and the function of
religion is to allow us to take a break from the moral struggle. It
grants us a moral holiday.

I have mentioned that one can find some rather half-hearted
supernaturalism in James – though it is to be offset by his naturalistic
explanations of religious phenomena such as conversion – but the
themes I have singled out are the striking ones, and very remarkable
they are. Few writers on religion can have gone so far in rejecting
asceticism and identifying the religious impulse with the will to live
and enjoy life. Faith has had many antonyms, and one could write a
history of it in terms of that to which it is seen as being opposed. But

THE MIRROR OF THE SOUL

surely nobody before James' generation could have said that faith is the opposite of anhedonia, incapacity for pleasure.

Yet James was of the post-darwinian generation, and so up-to-date that we even find him in the *Varieties* discussing Nietzsche. For him religion had to be about life's own joyous self-affirmation. At the time when he was delivering in Edinburgh the Gifford Lectures which provide the text of the *Varieties* he was approaching sixty, and had already suffered a serious heart incident. Yet no shadow falls across its pages. He speaks of soul-sickness – such as in earlier years he had known himself – with his own unfailingly robust intelligence and good humour. He makes one wonder what optimism is, and how it came about that in the nineteenth century so many leading artists and thinkers were markedly either optimists or pessimists. Could there be reasons for being one or the other, and if it is a good thing to be optimistic, just how are religious belief and practice supposed to help one to become so?

Let us begin with the problem of reasons. The human condition just is what it is. We know of no other way that things ever were, nor can we think through very satisfactorily how things might be different, either radically better or worse, while yet we ourselves remain as we now are. But if things just are what they are, and we know no other condition of things, then there is no basis for any general judgment about life, whether favourable or unfavourable, for there is nothing to compare it with. We are thus left with an uncomfortable suspicion that the entire philosophy of life of great thinkers such as Freud, Kierkegaard and Schopenhauer is ultimately determined by non-rational factors. Reasons are certainly produced – but then, we know that clever people can and do think up reasons for almost any view of life. Are we to say then, as Nietzsche said, that every philosophy is just an expressive spiritual autobiography whose deepest foundations are non-rational choices of attitude?

James can admit this, because his pragmatism is not so far from Nietzsche's nihilism and voluntarism. (They *both* much admired R. W. Emerson!) James is saying that where the ultimate questions of life are concerned we find that over large areas arguments are either lacking or inconclusive. In such areas we are entitled to choose for ourselves what faith to live by. And by what criterion shall we choose? Since it is our philosophy of *life* that is in question, we should choose that faith which we find to be most life-enhancing.

Thus, with respect to supernatural belief, it is life-enhancing to feel that one's own life is umbilically connected to, throbs in unison with and is part of some great and everlasting Whole. The pluralistic pantheism of James' later thought enables us to feel that the whole universe is a kind of federal republic, an extension of the American Dream. And it is good, too, to feel every morning and every springtime how life continually renews itself. That fresh surge of life and *bonhomie* simply *is* religion, and we are entitled to adopt the beliefs, practices and allegiances that best charge us up with it. So says James.

Why *religion*, though? Would not a work-out in the gymnasium do as well? Like many philosophers, James is hazy about precisely which religious practices should be followed, and why. Few people, indeed, have ever tried to explain to us just how religious practices may help us to realize religious values. We are told to do these things, but not told exactly why, nor how they are supposed to work. No doubt James wishes to leave such questions open, since within his scheme of things there is place for a great variety of religions; but we are still left to decide how the pursuit of life, happiness and social well-being is to be reconciled with other values. For example, I have often felt a sinking of the heart when people begin a sentence, 'I like to think that . . .', and go on to talk of dead relatives who look down on them from heaven, of reincarnation, of life after death for animals, or whatever. Are there any limits at all here, or should we look equally sympathetically and encouragingly at any belief whatever that people may adopt in order to keep their spirits up?

There is a question here about the limits of intellectual permissiveness in matters concerning which none of us really knows the answers, a question that also arises in relation to some of the new happiness- religions. To a spiritually disorientated and lonely person a group like the Rajneesh Movement may seem very attractive. Its beliefs are less obviously absurd than those of many other religions, and it emphasizes vitality and self-expression. The adherents appear to be busy and happy. Does not this meet the Jamesian criteria? I have no views about the Rajneesh Movement in particular, but one can well imagine that there may be a movement of that kind with only one drawback: that to join it you know you must give up that unique inner kernel of loneliness, scepticism and freedom that you cherish most of all. Are you willing?

If on reflection you find that you cannot give that thing up, then

Jamesian well-being, sociability and life-affirmation are not after all your most important religious values. There is something else that matters more: spiritual freedom, even when it is anti-social or pessimistic.

3

Freud I

Sigmund Freud was born in Moravia in 1856, the first child of a middle-class Jewish family.[7] His father was in his 40s; his mother only 21. It seems that Freud senior's religion, though not non-existent, was so liberal that the son could think of himself as having had a non-religious upbringing.

In 1860 the family moved to Vienna, and Freud grew up in a society that was Imperial, Catholic and anti-semitic. He always saw himself as an outsider struggling for recognition, identifying himself with figures like Moses or Hannibal whom he saw as having conquered from without.

At school he discovered and instantly accepted darwinism. In 1873 he enrolled as a medical student, and from 1876 to 1882 worked as an assistant to a well-known Professor in the Institute of Physiology. His first publications were in the field of anatomy and physiology, and he obtained his MD in 1881, a dozen years later than William James.

Next year his ambition, always strong, was further fired by his engagement to Marthe Bernays. In 1885 he became a *privatdozent*, a sort of freelance tutor at the University, and soon afterwards was able to visit Paris to study under Charcot and see the use of hypnosis to treat hysteria. In 1886 he married, and set up in private practice; but for nearly twenty years money would continue to be short, and patients were often too few.

In his research Freud was working during the years 1886 to 1893 on neurology, and especially the cerebral palsies of children. Out of this work, still very much in the field of orthodox medicine, grew the unpublished and unfinished *Project for a Scientific Psychology* (1895), now regarded as one of his most important writings. It proposes an 'economic' model of the mind as a system of channels and of energies seeking discharge through them. Battling with this essay, Freud discovered the limits of a mechanistic model of the mind and, it seems, was therefore obliged to seek out more adequate metaphors.

At any rate, from 1892 in treating hysterias he had already abandoned hypnosis and instead adopted Breuer's 'cathartic method'. To it he added the use of free association as a tool of enquiry. In 1893 and 1895 he and Breuer produced two joint works on the new technique. The first described the trauma theory of hysteria, and the second reported the phenomenon of transference.

From this time Freud's theoretical creativity, the rate at which he devised new interpretative concepts, was very high: defence, repression, the neurosis as a compromise-formation produced by conflict between the ego and libido, the term 'psychoanalysis' – the new ideas came tumbling out. From 1897 Freud's self-analysis involved a study of dreams which led him to abandon the trauma theory and substitute the ideas of infantile sexuality and the Oedipus complex. In 1900 *The Interpretation of Dreams* announced the dynamic theory of mental processes, the notion of the unconscious, and the dominance of the pleasure-principle. Further major additions to the growing body of theory came in 1905, when in *Three Essays on the Theory of Sexuality* Freud published his complex genetic theory of the development of sexuality.

In 1906, when he reached his fiftieth birthday, there were at last some signs of recognition. The small group of his followers gathered and presented him with a commemorative medal inscribed with the line about Oedipus: 'Who solved the riddle of the Sphinx, and was the wisest of men'. Freud was pleased by this; and he was further gratified to receive at last the title of Professor. Soon he was to be joined by the brilliant young Swiss psychiatrist C. G. Jung. The First International would meet in 1908, and in 1909 Freud was to accept an invitation to lecture in the United States.

From 1891 to 1939 Freud's home and consulting rooms were in the same apartments in the Berggasse, Vienna. He may not have been quite so monumental a character as some have made out, but his way of life was on the whole very disciplined, uneventful and productive. His work as the founder of a growing international movement and as a prolific creative thinker and writer was carried out in addition to the many hours of every day that were spent in treating patients.

By 1910 or so the doctrines of classical psychoanalysis were complete. Freud would often explain them by going over the story of how they had been reached, a story that began not with his own work but with Breuer's use of 'the talking cure', the cathartic method.

Breuer had had a patient who had fallen into hysteria after nursing her much-loved father on his deathbed. The condition was severe, giving rise to paralysis and acute problems of sight and speech. However, Breuer noticed her muttering a few words in English.[8] Building on this with the help of hypnosis, he persuaded her to elaborate her fantasies, which began from her situation by the deathbed. After talking a while, she felt better, and Breuer noticed after several such sessions that the more emotion she expressed, the greater the subsequent improvement. Furthermore, her symptoms turned out to be related to past painful moments when she had been forced to bottle up her feelings because of her nursing duties.

Interpreting this anecdote, Freud comments that hysterical patients suffer from memories, their symptoms being like monuments to past *traumatic* experiences to which their mental life has become *fixated*. The traumas had been *pathogenic*, emotion long *repressed* having been *converted* into the symptoms. But the patient herself was *unconscious* of her true condition, and needed the help of the physician to *discharge* the repressed emotion and ideas.

In this account we notice the influence of the economic model of the self as a system of forces and channels, on which Freud was currently working. There is a strikingly Newtonian idea, the conservation of repressed psychic energy. But more important, and easily missed, is the fact that Freud is a writer who seeks *le mot juste*, the illuminating metaphor, and is very good at finding it.

More metaphors were quickly added. The patient did not remember the moments by the deathbed which had been so traumatic, and Freud postulated *resistance* as the force which was preventing the buried memories from rising into consciousness. But what had buried them in the first place? They had been *repressed* because they were too painful, and Freud as a good darwinian[9] realizes that the repression and the subsequent resistance must have biological functions. They are *defence mechanisms*. But why defences against simple love and grief, which are perfectly healthy and creditable feelings? Freud guesses that some much more serious threat to self-esteem must be involved. Consider cases where a person says, 'I could not live with myself if I were to do such a thing', or where shame drives a person to suicide. Do not such cases show that the maintenance of our ethical self-respect is vital to us?

So Freud suspects that at the moment of trauma the hysterical patient becomes aware of a morally intolerable wish and at once represses it. The patient's ethical standards are the repressing forces; and Freud describes another case, that of a girl attracted to her own elder sister's husband. The sister fell mortally ill, and the girl nursed her. The moment the elder sister died, the thought leapt into the girl's mind: 'Now he is free, and can marry me!'; and for the first time she realized that she had wished for her own sister to die. The thought was instantly repressed, and the girl fell into hysterical illness, in which she lost all memory of the scene by the bedside. Under treatment she was able to recall the memory with violent emotion, and recovered.

Freud is an insistent cacangelist, a bringer of bad news. With Marx and Nietzsche he is called one of 'the masters of suspicion', because he has such a nose for our self-deceptions, and such a determination to expose them.

He continues to elaborate the situation we have described: if the patient has become neurotic, then the repression has not been wholly successful. Something has escaped. How? Evidently the repressed feeling or wish has continued to exist unconsciously, and has contrived to get out, manifesting itself in disguised form as the symptom. The symptom is a sign or symbol: it obliquely alludes to the trauma, as Lady Macbeth's handwashing gestures express in symbolic form both her sense of guilt and her desire to be purged of it.

It now seems that the neurotic illness has itself a biological function. The patient needs the illness, for its symptoms are symbolic outlets for intensely painful feelings that must find expression, and cannot yet get out in any other form. In therapy the physician seeks to open the valve. The symptom must be analysed and decoded so that we may know the truth about what is behind it.

The moment when the hitherto-repressed feeling or wish is finally exposed and brought into full consciousness is like the recognition-scene in a Greek tragedy. Inevitably, and healthily, there is a violent discharge of emotion. But now the patient has been persuaded to surrender the obscure comfort of illness in favour of the daylight of self-knowledge. He has stepped out of Plato's Cave. His forbidden wish, when it is at last understood, is not so terrifying after all. There is something pathetically human about it. Named, it can be coped with.

In the early 1900s Freud would often speak of himself as seeking to gain knowledge of the unconscious mind. This idea is itself a metaphor, and one that has been much criticized. Freud seems to be postulating a metaphysical entity, by definition inaccessible even to the subject to whom it belongs, and then to be claiming to be able to collect information about it. Much better to formulate his discovery in other terms: Freud showed that large areas of our mental life and of our behaviour are symbolic, in ways of which hitherto we had been largely unaware. Examples include dreams, faulty or haphazard actions, mannerisms and jokes, as well as neurotic symptoms.

Freud thought that dreams were particularly valuable because repression is lower in sleep. It is not wholly absent, for the censor still usually prohibits any too naked an expression of our wishes. But because dreams provide us with an abundance of material that is a little easier to decode, we can use them in order to learn the psyche's natural logic and its natural symbolic language.

Both points are important. To understand a dream demands more than a simple interpretation of each successive symbol that occurs in the dream. We need to understand the logic of the dream-work, the complex process by which the dream-thoughts are transformed into the manifest content of the dream.

Freud's enquiries early led him to the conclusion that the sources of neurosis are usually, if not invariably, in the erotic life. Analysis repeatedly finds itself travelling back through puberty to early infancy, because Freud maintains that repressed childish erotic wishes are alone of sufficient power to construct lasting symptoms. Freud taught not only that the infant is a sexual being, but that the sexual and related feelings of infancy are the most powerful feelings we ever have, and the most lasting in their effects. A human being seems to come into the world as a tightly-coiled spring that is suddenly released. Most of its locked-up emotional energy is dissipated very quickly, and thereafter the unwinding becomes slower and slower. Adulthood is sluggish in the extreme, compared with the intense passions of childhood.

The doctrine is a very remarkable one, and we note the parallel between this view of the self and our 'Big Bang' cosmology. In both the self and the universe the really high energy-level is at the beginning, and thereafter there is a gradual unwinding and cooling down.

To explain his theory of sexuality Freud was obliged to widen the common understanding of the word. As everywhere in biology, the specialized develops from the generalized. Adult sexual feeling and behaviour is heteroerotic and characterized by genital primacy and a reproductive aim. But this biologically specialized behaviour has evolved from something that in the infant is less clearly defined. In its earliest stages infantile sexuality is more like what most people would call sensuality. It is dominated by the pleasure-principle, auto-erotic, and polymorphously perverse, in that sensual pleasure is obtained through the whole skin surface, through sucking, through excretion and so on. Adult sexuality is attained only as the terminus of a long process of development during which the various components of the sex-drive are organized towards the goal of heterosexual genital union.

Because the process is so complex, Freud's theory of sexual development provides him as a corollary with a comprehensive theory of the principal neuroses in terms of their sexual aetiology. Each main kind of neurosis or personality-disorder may be regarded as resulting from a disturbance at some specific stage in the development, which has caused a malformation or a fixation at that stage. Furthermore the varieties of normal adult sexual behaviour, courtship and play – including such acts as kissing – can be seen as recapitulating our sexual development.

Freud further remarks that the instinctual components of the sex-drive, libido, come in pairs of opposites, positive and negative. These include love and hatred, tenderness and violence, sadism and masochism, voyeurism and exhibitionism, perversion and neurosis. Although the term Oedipus complex was not used in print until 1910, Freud had been suggesting for some years beforehand that the infant has highly ambivalent feelings towards his parents and siblings. He loves and wishes to be loved, but he also feels jealousy, fear and hatred. In the four-year-old boy Oedipal wishes are balanced by castration-anxiety, and his further personal development depends upon the successful resolution of this conflict.

From all this it is clear that in Freud's view of life the self occupies a

no-man's-land, an uncomfortable frontier-zone between the insistent demands of our biological drives and the restraints imposed
upon us by society and its ethical standards. Culture is inescapably
repressive: we cannot be socialized without some pain. But most
adults find ways of coping. They either achieve their desires, or give
them sublimated expression, or indulge them in fantasy and dreams.
The neurotic, however, are not strong enough to cope, and fall victim
to pressures that others manage to endure. The flight into illness does
give some satisfaction, and the neurotic person may be expected to
cling to his or her symptoms until offered something preferable. It is
noticeable that the flight to illness often takes the form of regression
to an infantile condition of sexual life, in disguise.

Psychoanalysis is not socially subversive, as so many of its critics
allege, says Freud. On the contrary, it is the ally of civilization, for its
aim is to help people to accept the demands of society. By making our
rebelliousness conscious the therapist makes it manageable. But
when Freud says this he makes his modern readers aware of an irony,
for today he is commonly charged with being all too conservative,
and especially with encouraging his women patients to reconcile
themselves to conditions they ought rather to have changed.

The later development of psychoanalytical theory is a very
complex story. Two ideas only need be singled out here.

In 1923 Freud first uses the triad of terms, Superego, Ego and Id as
a kind of mnemonic formula summarizing his view of the personality. Almost all the ideas involved go back some twenty-five years or
more, and the new formula should not be read too literally, as if it
defined three parts or three levels within the soul. It is rather an
interpretative device, a useful tool.

The Superego is the heir of the Oedipus complex, the conscience. It
embodies the standards we set for ourselves. It should not be self-
punishing but should have become detached from the father, cool,
impersonal and universal. According to Freud a religious conscience,
in which the believer remains subject to the father-god, is an
imperfectly-formed conscience, still immature and not as autonomous as it should have become. In Freud the idea of God is always
objectified and anthropomorphic, and he never considered the
possibility of religious internalization. He describes very well how
we are to come to a mature relationship to our earthly fathers, but he
does not consider that we might follow a similar path in coming to an
adult relationship with the heavenly father. My god must be

internalized to become my own non-objectified, cool, inward and rationally-chosen religious ideal, my spiritual guiding principle. In both cases, the case of the earthly father and the case of God, it is important to escape from domination by the objective being, and to do it not by revolt but by appropriating the values and standards the being embodies for us. When we have made fully our own all that by which they have authority over us, then they no longer impose upon us, because they are no longer objective.

The Ego, as we have seen, is the product of the conflict between the pleasure-principle and the reality-principle, the demands of the Id and the inhibitions necessary to social life. Freud follows the Nietzschean maxim that punishment is the creator of consciousness: the Ego is awakened precisely by the constant buffeting it receives from both sides, and has the task of continually arbitrating between them.

Our chief doubt about this is that it leaves us asking why have not more animals of other species also become conscious? There are many species of mammal who live in troupes and whose young males must spend many years under the domination of the older males before at last they can overthrow and displace them. As everybody knows, Freud himself suggests that the first human beings lived in a society of this type, so he clearly regards such a social structure as favourable to the creation of consciousness, and also of religion and morality. But if it did the trick for us, why for us alone? Why not also for many other species of baboon, monkey and ape? The answer is presumably that in the case of man the conflict between the demands of the Id and the constraints of society is exceptionally severe. This may be true: there is, for example, no animal baby whose emotional distresses are as intense and heart-rending as those of human babies. But why? We will offer a suggestion shortly.

Finally, the Id is the cluster of primary instinctual drives by which our psychic life is powered. Freud emphasizes that they do not form a system, but aim independently each for its own satisfaction, and may often conflict with each other. If this language is to be taken at face value, and the drives really are independent of each other, then it ought to be possible to give an accurate list of them. But Freud never systematized his answer to this question, and various lists are given. The drives commonly include self-preservation, aggression, the need to be loved and protected, the need for pleasure/pain, the sex drive, and even a drive for death and destruction. But one may well ask from a strictly darwinian point of view, what can be the biological advantage of having such an anarchic and potentially self-destructive apparatus? Once again, animals seem to be much cooler than we are – or is it that Freud's mythology is influenced by a nineteenth-century picture of nature as being 'bestial'; savage, disorderly, and red in tooth and claw?

In 1925 there was an important reversal in Freud's interpretation of anxiety. He had always been aware that there are two main types of anxiety. As well as the neurotic anxiety which is typically an expression of sexual frustration, there is also a healthy and realistic kind of anxiety which on the basis of past experience warns us to avoid what is likely to be disagreeable. But for many years neurotic anxiety attracted all the attention, with the doctrinal disputes about whether or not one accepted an exclusively sexual aetiology of the neuroses. When that issue had cooled down it became easier to acknowledge that proper theoretical priority ought now to be given to the normal, biological-valuable kind of anxiety, and Freud thought of reversing his original order of things. Anxiety is basic in the psychic economy, and it is not sexual repression that produces anxiety but rather, anxiety that produces sexual repression.

This important theoretical shift suddenly brought psychoanalysis close to existentialist philosophy, which had been saying since Kierkegaard that the primal human response to our human condition is one of anxiety or dread. The existentialists interpret this anxiety as being a fear of one's own existence as solitary, free, finite, as-yet-unformed, caught between spiritual contradictions and confronted by death and nothingness. Freud's more clinical analysis suggests that the fear of separation from the mother gives rise to hysteria, the fear of castration to the various phobias, and the fear of the loss of the superego's approval to obsessional neurosis.

Incidentally, the loss of the approval of the superego or the parents is the most serious matter of all. It creates a threat of absolute rejection or exclusion, and therefore of death. Hence the affinity in religious thought between death and condemnation.

These considerations suggest that the furious despair of the baby's scream, referred to earlier, expresses a primal rage against the conditions of human existence and whoever or whatever has imposed them. From the first the infant discovers himself to be in a hopelessly and humiliatingly dependent and vulnerable situation, and it is not many years before he grasps that these conditions will return in a much worse form towards the end of life, when the *best* that people can hope for is a long-drawn-out decline. So the primal infantile response to life is one of helpless – and potentially self-destructive – anger.

This may cast a new light on the function of belief in the caring Providence of a good and loving God. Claims that this belief can be rationally inferred from the way life is and the way the world works may be mystifying reversals of the truth. It may rather be a corrective idea, needed not because of its own merits, but in order to counteract the *opposite* belief. When human beings are first confronted with the conditions of human existence, they respond by assuming that God must be malignant, and they rage against him accordingly. But however natural it may be, such a mood is self-destructive. We gain nothing by spending our lives in a state of *saeva indignatio*, raging against the dying of the light. It poisons the soul, and indeed in extreme cases has deprived people of their sanity. For our own well-being we need to be persuaded that life is sweet and God is good.

4

Freud II

Freud's view of the relation of nature to society was in many ways as close to Aristotle's as to ours. Nature was wild, irrational and antisocial. Like a horse or a vine it needed to be trained and domesticated. As reason by itself cannot move anything but must harness the passions, so society needs the energy of the instinctual drives, but must find ways to tap it and divert it so as to make it run along new and more useful channels.

On Freud's account we are fundamentally anti-social beings, and the development of social life has demanded a progressive renunciation, or at least a redirection, of our instinctual wishes. Has it been worth it, and how have we been persuaded or compelled to co-operate?

There are four basic means by which society secures instinctual renunciation in its members. It may simply enforce *frustration*, but people can only bear so much. It may offer opportunities of *sublimation*, by which the instincts can be redirected towards creative and socially-approved ends, but only a minority of people are really happy with sublimated gratifications. Thirdly, as a cool and anxiety-free morality becomes more widespread, it makes possible the *rational rejection* of our anti-social wishes. But this attitude will also be for the few only. We are left with the old fall-back, *repression*, demanded of us by the great controlling institutions of the law, morality and public opinion, and religion, all of which are old, wise and powerful and have many ways of inducing us to stay in line.

However, even repression has its limits, and creates a number of rebels and casualties. Freud favoured a very modest relaxation of repression, to reduce the casualties; but he was distinctly conservative by today's standards. In sexual morality, for example, he was opposed to masturbation, prostitution and homosexuality, and in the main held views quite close to those of the modern Roman Catholic Church.

Yet he taught 'the dominance of the pleasure principle', which means that he was a psychological hedonist who held that all our motivating drives blindly and urgently seek the pleasure of their own gratification. If indeed we desire pleasure above all, how have we been induced to accept the demands of civilization?

Freud's answer is that life is so hard and full of pain that in practice the avoidance of pain takes priority over the pursuit of pleasure; and although civilization does not deliver very much intense pleasure, it is very good indeed at minimizing uncertainty, discomfort and pain. Chaste monogamy is less stressful than adultery, and experience teaches that the renunciation of wayward desire and absorption in work gives a better balance of pleasure over pain than does libertinism. Such is the sober meaning of Freud's well-known recipe for a good life, 'love and work'.

Freud notes that the terms of the bargain are somewhat different for different strata of society. The dominant groups in society are very often required to pay a higher price in that they have to keep up appearances and, in many cases, to accept the constraints of a professional code; but at the same time they are well placed to ensure that they get the lion's share of the benefits. Sombrely, Freud points out that his own clientele proves that there is a great deal of frustration and dissatisfaction even among the most privileged, the leisured class. This suggests that there are narrow limits to what society can ever hope to deliver in the way of personal happiness; and yet the fact is that civilization can hope to survive only if the majority of people have an interest in its survival because they are getting a decent share of its benefits.

That is the nearest Freud comes to socialism. Less optimistically, he holds that because our emotional constitution is erotic and works in terms of domination and submission we will never be fully capable of anarchism or even republicanism. Man is not a herd animal but a horde animal, and there cannot be a stable fraternal society of co-operating pairs of mutually-contented couples. For any group to cohere, some erotic energy must be siphoned off and expended on hero-worship of the group-leader. The people are then held together by their common erotic subjection to him. Thus around the world today monarchy is in most places abolished and yet, whatever the local politics, there will be found a leader who personifies the state and who is erotically dominant as old-bull-male, wise-mother or dashing-younger-man. Social cohesion still as much as ever depends upon political-erotic subjection (although in our modern debate there is more attention to the politics of sexuality than to the sexuality of politics). But Freud is willing, whether consistently or not, to voice the hope that one day there may be a dictatorship of reason to replace the present system.

In his view of the human condition Freud nowhere allows himself to be optimistic or perfectibilist. He was born in a century which had first developed a harsh view of nature, and then had locked man into it. Inevitably, he was led to take an historical and tragic view of the self as inexorably bound by the necessities of nature and of its own past, while at the same time he was also a scientific rationalist determined to expose and face the facts of human irrationality. The human condition was girt about with limitation, suffering, transience and death, but dreams of escaping from the prison were as futile as making complaints about it. Freud's spirituality requires us to eschew dreams of salvation, rationally to accept the facts of the human condition, to absorb ourselves as far as we can in human love and hard creative work, and above all never, ever, to complain.

What Freud has to say about the forms of religion that he rejects is voluminous, varied and sometimes sharp. He is pretty good on the emotional dynamics of the naïver kinds of patriarchal monotheism – though not so very good, because he does not have the insight or the sympathy of a Feuerbach. However, Freud's own personal religion-less religion, his stoical spirituality, is much more interesting and important than his critique of Christianity. Are the facts of the human condition here correctly described, and is this the one and only rational and practicable response to them? – Always bearing in mind, of course, that the very notion that there is a set of objective, unalterable and constraining 'facts of the human condition' may itself be questionable.

Freud's stance needs to be distinguished from that of certain close neighbours, of whom the chief is Schopenhauer. Freud's own naturalism was scientific: that is, he was a realist about scientific knowledge, and also a determinist. Hence the prison bars. But Schopenhauer was a Kantian, who took a constructivist view of scientific knowledge as being mere 'representation', an ordering of appearances; so that Schopenhauer's naturalism could not be quite the same as Freud's. Nevertheless, Schopenhauer's metaphysics of the will anticipates in a remarkable manner the mood of the later post-darwinian and biological type of naturalism, so that Schopenhauer was in many ways the first modern pessimistic unbeliever, and the one who set the tone for generations to come.

How was Schopenhauer able to be a determinist, if the ordering of our knowledge in terms of cause and effect is ideal, something done by the mind? In such a case, as with Kant, the determinism could surely be no more than phenomenal? The answer to this seems to be the same for Schopenhauer as it is for Nietzsche in his 'positivist' period: the world is indeed everlastingly mere chaos, a formless and meaningless flux of becoming, but in that flux, as in the equally formless and ungovernable sea, there is an ineluctable necessity that carries all before it. Schopenhauer anticipates Freud and many another in his sense of the dark, unfeeling and unloving powers that govern human destiny, of the relative impotence and insignificance of the conscious self in the face of the forces of nature without and within it, and of the incurability of the human condition.

However, Schopenhauer is very exceptional among Western thinkers in recommending something very like the Buddha's response. Whether his doctrine of salvation has any content is questionable: even at the very end of his great book we still cannot tell whether Schopenhauer's Nirvana is or is not simple extinction. When he declares that 'to the world the saints are nothing; but then, to the saints the world is nothing', we are uncomfortably aware that the same might as well be said of the dead. Does Schopenhauer's doctrine differ in the end from that of those pessimists in the *Greek Anthology* who say that non-existence is preferable to life?

At any rate, Freud had no truck with such a view. Everywhere one is aware of the strength of his sense of biological reality, and a biologist simply does not dwell on pessimistic thoughts by way of getting us into the mood of preferring extinction to life. Nor, secondly, was Freud nostalgic for any older world-view that he sees as a lost paradise, in the manner of so many English writers from Hardy to Philip Larkin and beyond. He is unimpressed by those mystical or oceanic states in which the soul regresses to a primordial watery unity, and equally unseduced by any hankering after the innocent faith of the nursery.

Freud not only rejected any turning away from the facts of life towards asceticism, mysticism or childlike faith, but he also rejected the superabundant life-affirmation of the Nietzschean Superman. He will not allow even an intra-mundane and naturalistic form of salvation. He seeks to persuade us that we are all, every one of us, in some degree chronically sick — and, therefore, paradoxically, that we must at last finally abandon the quest for a panacea. As Philip Rieff has observed, 'In the emergent democracy of the sick, everyone can to some extent play doctor to others, and none is allowed the temerity to claim that he can definitively cure or be cured. The hospital is succeeding the church and the parliament as the archetypal institution of Western culture.'[10]

Even in 1959 Rieff allowed a whiff of irony in those words, as if he already realized even then that Freud had not discovered ancient facts and necessities, but had created new ones. Nature is a social creation, seen quite differently in different cultures and periods. Freud did not find out that we are caged: he made that cage, and almost got away with throwing away the key. His thought is a great tower of metaphors, and those metaphors are indeed quantitative and mechanistic. But no neurophysiologist has put electrodes on anybody's head and detected the physical quantities that correspond to repressed feelings, biological drives and all the rest. The brilliant system is a work of art, a hermeneutic, constructed to persuade us to adopt Freud's view of life. It does not justify the spirituality; rather, one suspects that it is an expression of the spirituality.

Feminism helped us to see this. Freud's teaching suggested that, for each individual, coming to terms with his or her own sexuality was almost life's chief task. A strong patriarchal conservative, he thought culture should reinforce heterosexuality by heightening gender-contrasts and polarizing the sexes. This teaching deflected women away from seeking political and economic emancipation and towards the pursuit of sexual fulfilment, especially in the period around 1925–1965. But when feminism reasserted itself and Freud's texts were re-read in the light of it, it became clear how much of his thought was an ideology of male supremacy. He himself seemingly never realized how vulnerable to this criticism he would one day appear. 'Anatomy is destiny' (scilicet, and therefore women must resign themselves to inferiority) was a classic case of a social institution attempting to justify itself by appeal to alleged unalterable natural facts.

Similar manoeuvres pervade Freud's system. I asked at the beginning if Freud's account of the human condition justifies the impressive stoic spirituality that he deduces from it. The answer seems to be that the system, and all the supposed unalterable facts of nature and the human condition, are expressions of the spirituality. Here, as we found with William James, the choice of one's basic view of life – optimistic or pessimistic, religious or non-religious, naturalistic or world-denying – seems to be primal and to determine everything else: yet in itself it remains a mystery. When did we make that choice, from which so much else has flowed?

5

Psychological Man

Like the music of Claude Debussy, the later thought of C. G. Jung is an endless winding self-absorbed reverie, a contemplation of the unfolding life of his own psyche.[1] Did he really discover buried within it a universal key to the imaginative and religious life of all humanity, or was he simply mulling over the fruits of his own extensive and curious learning? Was it all genuinely innate – or merely acquired? The former, he said, believing that his own rich psychic life was not a rarity. Perhaps he attracted people like himself or perhaps he used his dominant personality to impose his own interpretations upon them, but at any rate it seemed to him that his patients were giving him independent confirmation of his discoveries, and not just obediently echoing his own opinions.

The psyche, Jung held, was boundless. Its world was the eternal and imperishable world of religion. It bore within the collective unconscious a huge reservoir of all the imaginative and spiritual capacities that have found such varied expression in the cultural life of mankind. Everybody carries within himself the universal human, and therefore possesses an organ of universal communication. The psyche was retrospectively unbounded, and one could go back through the personal and the collective unconscious into the darkness of the biological and even the mineral life from which we have come forth. Thus through the psyche Jung could commune with nature and with his own ancestors. Furthermore, the psyche knows nothing of death: to enter into it was to escape from the tyranny and the terror of our linear clock-time, and to re-enter the golden, endless time-out-of-time of myth, childhood and religion.

Jung's use of his psyche as an organ of intuitive understanding, a way of gaining insight into highly exotic materials, was undoubtedly effective. However we interpret his language about the psyche (and it is certainly puzzling), if the new ways of thinking that he sought to introduce – or should it be, the old ways of thinking that he sought to revive? – are genuine, and really work, then Jung has changed our view of the human condition.

The reason for this is that ever since Galileo and Descartes, and certainly still in Freud's thinking, human life has been seen as more or less completely subject to the mechanistic metaphysics they introduced. Our life was seen as a bodily life amidst a world of bodies moving about in Euclidean space and linear time, every event taking place in accordance with universal laws of nature. We were bound by time, by bodiliness and by the law of cause and effect. Yet Jung was attempting to demonstrate that the more important part of our life is lived outside these constraints.

In this he was of course campaigning against what he saw as Freud's reductive dogmatism, and his method owed much to Kant. Kant had sought 'to destroy knowledge in order to make room for faith', which meant that he sought to restrict the application of Newtonian scientific ideas of space, time, matter and causal determination to the sphere of empirical knowledge, and thereby to save the greater and more important moral sphere of life from being threatened by them. Along rather similar lines, Jung would allow that for various practical purposes within life we need to make use of ideas of linear clock-time, an objective physical order of things, and the complete determination of all events by antecedent efficient causes. There is no doubt that, in their place, such ideas are useful. But Jung wanted to show that our inner life is not wholly subject to them; and if he is correct in this claim, then that is an important matter. Freudians may mutter darkly about 'psychotic traits' and 'withdrawal from reality' – as they do, because Jung catches them on the raw – but they will mutter in vain, because Jung will have overcome their definition of reality. He will have changed the rules, not broken them.

Jung did not wish to see our modern scientific-industrial civilization overthrown, for he knew it was here to stay. But, in the great Kantian tradition, he did wish to prevent its mechanistic metaphysics from imprisoning and destroying the human spirit. He aims therefore, by delimiting the scope of the mechanistic metaphysics, to allow the psyche room to breathe, to unfold itself and to affirm its own characteristic ways of thinking. It would scarcely be consistent with his own principles for him to set up his own system as a rival to Freud's, but he does have a distinctive point of view on all the chief topics in Freud's system. As we examine his divergence from Freud, we see how hard and consistently he battles to overcome the tyranny of time past and of mechanistic causation. Inevitably, he had to begin with the most important question of all, the characterization of the Unconscious mind and the way it functions.

The Freudian Unconscious was a seething cauldron of often-incompatible biological drives, together with repressed material from infancy. It has indeed its own logic, the primary processes, but there was no hope of ordering it creatively or of finding healing powers within it. One had simply to strike the best obtainable bargain between the demands of the Unconscious and the constraints of external reality. But on Jung's account, although some of our unconscious processes are like Freud's Id, others are constructive and creative. Where Freud was a strict mechanist who set out to explain psychic states solely in terms of their antecedent causes, Jung was a vitalist who explained many psychic processes in terms of the aims they were seeking to achieve. The psyche, for Jung, was teleological, immanently goal-seeking, in ways of which the conscious self was largely unaware. It was therefore necessary to listen to the psyche, to get into the right relation to it and to take its utterances — dreams, in particular — as oracles. For the psyche, being an organism, is self-regulating. If we deform it by imposing on it the alien requirements of science-based industrial culture, it will endeavour to heal itself. Its activity is restorative, and its messages are not mere monuments to past traumas, but pointers to our future spiritual development.

The Unconscious that seeks to communicate with us in dreams and in religious experience is variously described by Jung as the Shadow, as a Doppelganger, double or Alter Ego, or simply as an angel of the Lord. Both Freud and Jung seek to make the Unconscious bit by bit more conscious, but for opposite reasons: Freud, in order to control it better; Jung, in order to learn from it and gain psychic health.

The same contrast appears in Jung's treatment of the Personal Unconscious, which comprises all that about myself which I have wilfully pushed out of sight. It can be elicited by analysis, or simply by reflection on my own dreams and fantasies, and is detected in the form of the Complex. For Freud a complex is a pathological formation, but for Jung it can be the focus of a striving for health, sometimes even acquiring a voice of its own that demands attention.

Like Freud, Jung held that we are all originally and at a deep level bisexual, but again the thought is handled in a way very much his own. One of the basic unconscious contents in each of us is the image of the opposite sex – for men, the Anima. The anima is both individual and universal, and its function is compensatory: it checks my tendency to unbalanced sexual chauvinism. If I make my conscious male persona very masculine and hard, then my anima will tend to become more emotional and intuitive in order to counterbalance it. One of our chief tasks is to come to terms with this image of the opposite sex within us, and so realize the ideal of the Androgyne. Insofar as I can do that, I can attain a certain lightness, sovereignty and freedom of spirit, the magical qualities that the androgynous spirits have in Shakespeare's comedies.

Jung's introversion shows in the hint here that celibacy is higher than marriage, because the most important sexual relationship is the inner one with one's own anima. Note, too, that although both he and Freud see marriage as a four-person relationship, the identities of the two invisible partners are different in the two cases. For Jung they are the man's anima and the woman's animus; for Freud, the man's mother and the woman's father.

The search for totality in Jung's thought it most apparent in his treatment of the self. Within the psyche there are four basic functions, the sensory-perceptual, the thinking, the feeling-emotional and the intuitive. In most of us one of these is over-developed at the expense of the others in response to the demands of society. The conscious self which the individual comes to develop and to present to society is thus not a complete self, but merely a public image or mask, the Persona. What could not be incorporated into the persona has been thrust down into the Unconscious, where it has become part of the Shadow – and now it is clear that this doctrine has been developed as a polemic against Freud's. Freud seeks to strengthen the rational Ego's control over the Unconscious; Jung declares that this same rational Ego is a warped and diminished self that needs to be reunited with its own estranged elements. The psyche will not be satisfied with anything less than the full integration of all the elements of the personality. To this end, the little Ego must die in order that the greater Self can come to birth. The greater and fully-integrated Self may therefore be symbolized as a newborn Child, or as Christ.

Once again we see that where Freud follows the mainstream European tradition and seeks rational control and hierarchy, Jung seeks harmony and totality. Freud limited the function of psychotherapy to resolving conflicts and to giving the individual just enough strength to get through life without unbearable suffering. The instinctual drives whose pressure ultimately gives rise to suffering are in themselves inbuilt, insatiable and indestructible. The most one can hope to do is to make such adjustments as will minimize their potential for causing distress. Furthermore, Freud was chiefly interested in our very early life, to which he traced the sources of later psychic suffering. Jung, however, believed that personality-development continues throughout life, the religious need for integration becoming steadily more insistent as we grow older. In this respect, indeed, middle-age is for many people a second and spiritual adolescence.

In forwarding our spiritual development symbols play an essential part through their peculiar ability to attract and transmute libido. Libido is simply psychic energy, of which the sex-drive is part; and Jung has a story of a ritual he witnessed in Africa to illustrate his meaning here. In Spring the men of a certain agricultural people dig a hole in the ground and surround it with bushes. They then dance round it, thrusting their spears into it. The symbol is that of the Impregnation of Mother Earth. The function of the ritual is to attract sexual energy, and to transmute it for a cultural purpose, into the energy needed to work the land and grow the crops. Jung sees many rituals as working in this way: they employ symbols which summon psychic energy and then direct it towards the task in hand. The Transmutation of Libido through symbol and ritual is thus Jung's equivalent of the Freudian 'sublimation', but he refuses simply to accept Freud's vocabulary because he rejects the reductionist Freudian view that sexuality is always fundamental and that religion and other cultural concerns are mere substitutes for it. Our religious needs, for Jung, are as primal and insistent as any other needs.

The highest-level and most powerful of symbols are those which represent and facilitate individuation, the final integration of the personality. A symbol of this kind is called by Jung a Reconciling Symbol, and he finds it to be commonly linked with the number four rather than three. Such are the mandala, the square (room, piazza, prison cell, fourgated city, fourfold gospel), the diamond and the circle (often divided into quadrants: hot-cross-bun, clockface, round table, orrery). A particularly instructive Quaternity in Christianity is the Coronation of the Virgin, which represents the Assumption of the relatively feminine and earthy human soul into the lucid, pure masculine Trinity. Thus, towards the end of his life, Jung was able to salute the proclamation of the Dogma of the Corporal Assumption of the Blessed Virgin Mary, in the Encyclical *Humani Generis* (1950), as a vindication of his teaching.

It was also a striking example of the principle of significant coincidence that Jung called Synchronicity, and saw as violating the normal rules of cause and effect. There was no way in which obscure stirrings within Jung's own psyche could have directly influenced the development of dogma in the Roman Catholic Church. For that matter, there was no way in which Jung's personal breakdown and visions of cosmic destruction in 1913–1914 could have directly contributed to the outbreak of the First World War. But such analogies and affinities between events in the external world and events in the psyche, or between events in two or more different psyches, do nevertheless frequently occur – or so Jung claimed.

Unfortunately, at this point as at several others Jung seems to feel no urgent need to form a theory about the intriguing phenomenon that he claims to have discovered. He is content simply to regard it as helping to falsify the mechanist enemy. But this is not enough, and Jung's failure to elaborate considerably weakens his case. At the end of his life, toying with ideas of immortality, and holding that the psyche's life is in some sense outside clock-time, he appeals to the well-known observation that the psyche cannot believe in its own extinction. But Freud himself would allow that much: natural selection has so bred us that emotionally we do not give up easily. Life struggles to the last, and Jung will only be asserting something more than what Freud is perfectly prepared to allow if he amplifies his own claim and gives it some substantial theoretical content. But this he fails to do.

The same thing happens in the all-important matter of Jung's teleological and vitalist view of the psyche. All that Jung offers by way of explanation of how it can have come about that we have evolved such a psyche is his comparison of it with an organism which is self-regulating and strives to attain its own full development. But, alas, this invocation of biology is fatal to the argument. For as the great theoretical biologist August Weismann pointed out (*The Evolution Theory*, 1902), it is the germ cells which maintain the species, and natural selection's only interest in us lies in forming us to be effective carriers and prolific transmitters of the genetic material whose vehicles we are. The point is not a very comfortable one, but Freud at least did grasp it. Jung does not explain how natural selection can have operated to form us for the achievement of our psychic fulfilment *after* the stage at which we have passed on our germ cells. The metaphor of the psyche as an 'organism' that has so evolved that it will reach maturity and wisdom in old age is a very weak metaphor if there is no way in which such a mature psyche can reproduce itself, and even weaker when we recall that for almost the entire period of human evolution the average expectation of life was only about twenty years. Old age, together with whatever spiritual goods may be attainable in it, is not biologically natural to us, but rather is a modern cultural achievement.

Since Jung's stance is in any case one of opposition to Freud's radically biological view of the self, it would seem to be consistent with his general outlook that he should abandon biological talk and openly admit that 'the psyche' is really cultural. For the programme of freeing the psyche from the prison of the mechanistic metaphysics had the aim of proving that what is in human life cannot wholly be explained by the methods of the natural sciences, that we are formed at least as much by our cultural history as by our biological past, and that a human being's need for meaning and for value is as urgent and as fundamental to him as any of his more strictly biological needs. Jung's theoretical diffuseness and woolliness may even be seen as making the same point: he does not wish to impose upon us a new scientific system to replace the old.

So why not go further? Nietzsche, whose thought underlies the teaching of both Freud and Jung, was surely correct: the human mind is at bottom a set of capacities for coining metaphors, telling tales and generating and following rules. Together we evolve our cultures as vast systems of conventions, meanings, values, symbols and stories; and the psyche is nothing but culture internalized. For we all carry about with us both the universal creative capacities and a very large stock of cultural material, enough to enable us to connect up with any other human culture and its products. Any human being who has mastered one natural language is in principle capable of also learning any other.

Jung's psychologism, his tendency to turn all questions into psychological questions, may now be seen as one version of modern anthropocentrism, not in fact very different from the version that says that all questions can be turned into questions about language. For in modern culture we increasingly see the world about us as being simply our world, made by us out of rules and signs and meanings. Reality itself is conventional; everything emerges from within ourselves. The mystery of the psyche is the divine mystery of creativity. Jung's doctrine of the Archetypes further develops the same point, showing us that we have within ourselves a whole range of primal and universal forms of symbolic expression, and thereby assuring us of the unity of human nature and the mutual intelligibility of cultures. As for the religious idea of the integration of the personality or individuation, it corresponds in the new psychologized and anthropocentric culture to the older idea of gaining supernatural salvation by union with a metaphysical God. God symbolized the unity of culture, and indeed incorporated all the great cultural values within himself. Now, as Jung makes quite clear, he is internalized to become our god with a lower-case 'g', the Self. The Creator is within.

6

Testing the Theories

There have been many sorts of psychologist: literary ones like Shakespeare, religious ones like Augustine and philosophical ones like Nietzsche. James, Freud and Jung all had a scientific training and orthodox medical qualifications; they claimed to be scientific psychologists. Even though none of them actually made many measurements or performed many experiments, they had believed themselves to be propounding scientific theories that were well grounded in biological principles, clinical experience and published evidence. And if all this is so, then their theories ought to be capable of empirical testing.[12]

The likeliest method of testing will be to deduce an empirical prediction from one of the theories, and then to check to see whether the prediction is in fact fulfilled. The likeliest arena for such a test is the social psychology of religion. Social psychologists measure human beliefs, behaviour and experiences by various methods such as social surveys, field studies and experiments. The chief interest is differential, and the method statistical. Thus the social psychologist of religion will need to fix a definition of religion, to establish criteria of religiosity, and to measure just how much religiosity there is about. He or she will then ask how religiosity varies with other factors. This leads to the discovery of some significant correlations: for example, in Britain churchgoers are much more likely to be country people rather than city-dwellers, elderly rather than young adults, women rather than men, and middle class rather than working class. The psychologist may then devise a hypothesis to account for one of these correlations, and look for a way of testing it. For example, it is known that women tend to be more introverted and anxious than men, and more liable to suffer from feelings of guilt and inadequacy. Forms of religion that promise forgiveness and salvation may therefore be especially attractive to women.

From this hypothesis we deduce the prediction that the more salvationist the religious group, the more women will predominate among its membership. Is the prediction fulfilled? Yes, by and large it is; for the predominance of women is least among the Orthodox and the Catholics, and greatest among the most salvationist Protestant groups.

However, it is necessary to be cautious, for it is easy to think of many other reasons why a traditional comprehensive 'folk' type of church may have a more nearly equal ratio of the sexes in its congregations, whereas a more modern type of Protestant sect in an urban society may have a predominance of women. In such a society women by living longer in any case predominate heavily among the elderly. Furthermore, most women until recently were not in full time work, needed a respectable outlet for their energies, and were much more active than men in almost every kind of voluntary organization that grew up, indeed, largely to give them something to do. It may be that full-time work and feminism will shortly end the traditional predominance of women in many churches and chapels. Thus the fact that the prediction based on the greater-anxiety hypothesis turned out to be fulfilled by no means settles the question. We may go on to speculate that women have in the past been more introverted and anxious than men because society has in various ways put more severe pressure on women than on men; so much so that for many ordinary women until a few decades ago the chapel and the church were among the few social centres that they could go to on their own without eyebrows being raised. In which case the anxiety and the higher church attendance were both caused by a third factor, the social subjection of women.

Even this brief discussion has already suggested a number of important points. First, there are many different kinds of religion, and no one theory is likely to explain them all. Secondly, people are religious for different reasons and in many different ways. Thirdly, an empirical measurement may be over-determined; i.e., in accordance with what more than one theory has independently led us to expect. We need also to be wary of questions concerning the direction of causation. For example, a man I knew was very religious, but also anxious and guilt-ridden; but did religion make him guilty, did guilt drive him to religion, or was he caught in a vicious circle in which the causal arrow pointed both ways? And precisely how would one set about answering such a question?

Finally, and most important of all, it has become obvious that the social psychology of religion needs an historical perspective. Clearly it is necessary to appeal to history in order to explain the enormous differences in the religious situation in the USA, Ireland, France and Holland. But that is not all, for research in Britain and the USA has been generating a fairly substantial literature annually since the 1930s, a period long enough to provide us with evidence of long-term and large-scale religious change. The gradual decline in religious observance is the only one of these changes that has been much discussed, but the literature now also provides much evidence of other kinds of religious change. Sometimes the subject itself may have helped to bring about change. In America in the late 1940s much was heard about 'the authoritarian personality', as psychologists of religion showed that religious people tended to be more racially prejudiced, conservative in their political and social outlook, dogmatic about beliefs and values, pro-war and so on. For a generation, young trainees for the ministry learnt about all this and resolved to change it. There was a period in which liberal clergymen confronted conservative congregations, but more recent evidence suggests that the churches have to a considerable extent now liberalized their attitudes.

The upshot of this discussion is that already, whenever we hear any empirical finding quoted, we need to check the country it comes from and its date. It is no longer possible for psychologists to talk as if the study of human nature could be separated from the study of history. Human nature is an historical product. Even the way our visual system works is subject to historical change.

Is it not strange that so long after geology and biology introduced an historical dimension into natural science, scientists still to a very large extent retain their traditional anti-historical outlook?

They do so for the very good reason that they are afraid of history. It is corrosively sceptical, leading almost irresistibly to a relativist or perspectivist outlook, whereas nearly all scientists are keen realists. They do not wish to see the world reduced to a Buddhist flux in which nothing at all endures forever unchanged. Science finds it very difficult to look its own history in the face. However, history cannot be kept at bay merely by disregarding it, and in fact the reality of historical change now shows up unmistakably within the (often anti-historical) literature of social psychology.

As for James, Freud and Jung, they were very gifted people indeed, and well aware of the nature of history — and yet they still produced anti-historical theories about human nature, as if there were an unchanging order in human nature about which one could formulate ahistorical scientific theories. And it is not so. It is strange that neither James, nor Freud nor Jung betrays any awareness of something that they must on reflection all have known: that their own accounts of human nature would become period pieces, datable artefacts typical of the age and the cultural milieux from which they emerged. This is not, of course, in any way to disparage them, for each of them produced a vision of human nature that was, and remains, a considerable feat of the creative imagination. They have been so influential that Freud and Jung have both produced large numbers of people who exemplify their respective theories. Before Jung there were no Jungians, nor any people even remotely like Jungians; but since Jung there have been large numbers of Jungians. He helped to create a new kind of person, as also did Freud. As I have said, this is not in any way to disparage them; but our discussion does, I submit, show that a straightforward scientific test of the truth of their theories is unlikely to be forthcoming.

What then do we find? Various indices of religiosity may be used. Some are objective and of an institutional kind: the number of full-time religious professionals employed, the volume of published material about religion and its readership, and the size of the budgets of the churches. Some criteria are purely subjective, in that we have only people's claims on their own behalf and no objective check. They include people's personal religious beliefs, their religious experiences and their saying of private prayers, and on all three criteria scores are very high. In Britain, for example, around half the population claim to hold at least some orthodox beliefs, to have had religious experiences and to say private prayers at least sometimes.

The third group of indices of religiosity are the ones where we have the possibility of comparing people's claims on their own behalf with an objective count. These include church membership and church attendance. In both cases, it turns out, people exaggerate handsomely. In the Britain of the 1980s the number of people who claim they were in church last Sunday is double the number to be found there on a direct count.

The indices of religiosity, then, are of different kinds; but by and large they keep in step, and frequency of church attendance has in general been found to be a good all-round measure of religiosity.

The correlations established are mostly banal, merely confirming the opinion of common sense. For example, young children are very religious, but doubts set in during the junior years. The peak age for conversion is the mid-teens, and those who turn to religion then do so chiefly because it meets a felt cognitive need, the need here being not merely for such an explanation of life as might equally well be provided by science, but rather for a framework of purpose and value which will give the individual something to live for.

After adolescence, religiosity declines, and the least religious people are young married people aged thirty to thirty-five. Thereafter people become progressively more religious as they grow older, and the books commonly cite a 1949 report that 100 per cent of people over ninety describe themselves as 'certain of an after-life'.

The rising interest in religion in later life and its broadly favourable correlation with good mental health is a point in favour of Jung. In Freud's favour is a good deal of evidence that people's religious beliefs and attitudes reflect their early relations with their parents. Freud's mistake was to overlook the religious importance of the mother, even though he has a passage at the end of *Totem and Taboo* where he himself points out that the great mother-goddesses of remote antiquity present a difficulty for the theory that God is modelled on the father alone. The available empirical evidence suggests that we project attributes of both our parents on to God; and there are tendencies both to see God in the image of the opposite-sex parent, and to see God in the likeness of the preferred parent.

The psychology of religion has, oddly enough, not yet attempted to study its own effects on religion, but we may guess that the fact that we now know that our God is an ideal love-object, embodying our values and reflecting our feelings for our parents, will make us more aware than we used to be of the symbolic and expressive character of religious belief.

Finally there is of course the weighty statistical evidence of long-term religious decline. Recent work has shown the process going on in Asian religions as well as in the West; and everywhere the decline is most marked at the growth-points, so that we may presume that it will continue. Europe's experience suggests that the process is so relentless that whether State policy is pro-religious or anti-religious makes little difference. Acquaviva comments:

> From the religious point of view, humanity has entered a long night that will become darker and darker with the passing of the generations, and of which no end can yet be seen. It is a night in which there seems to be no place for a conception of God, or for a sense of the sacred, and ancient ways of giving significance to our own existence, of confronting life and death, are becoming increasingly untenable.[13]

That is putting it too mildly. One could perhaps put it better by saying that the threat of nuclear war is only a symbol of a worse spiritual disaster that now threatens us.

7

Ecstasy

Interest – and I mean, our special kind of interest – in mysticism and religious experience is a recent phenomenon.[14] It could scarcely have been felt before the time of Rousseau and Boswell, for consider what it involves. There is an early-Romantic desire to go beyond the ordinary bounds of experience and pass over into certain archaic and extraordinary states. There is, inevitably, psychological man's self-conscious attentiveness to anything unusual in his own mental life, his desire to watch his own responses. And there is a modern form of the ancient belief that any and every abnormal state of mind may be a case of spirit-possession or may offer a glimpse into a hidden and higher world; the modern form of this belief being that in a time when we no longer think that we can justify religious faith by reason there may instead be a mystical short cut to certainty that is supernatural, empirical and indubitable.

Before people became psychologically-minded the literature of mysticism did exist, but only a very few people thought it interesting. Gifted people like John Wesley, who for their own reasons needed to ferret it out, were able to do so; and to such a man there was also available a substantial Protestant literature of personal testimonies. But in Wesley's day there was no scholarly study of mysticism, no knowledge of its existence beyond the classical and European tradition, and very little reprinting of the Christian mystics. The subject was simply not thought important. Typically dismissive was H. L. Mansel, the Kantian philosopher of religion, who in his 1858

Bampton Lectures declares that Christianity is about obeying God's revealed will and loving your neighbour: it has nothing in common, he declares, with 'the diseased ecstasies of mysticism'.

The language may seem strong to us now, but it did not seem strong then. Christianity formerly seemed to be solidly established in the ordinary mundane sphere of reason and the will, in the realm of normal consciousness and everyday morality. Ecstasies were unnecessary, irrelevant and probably subversive. Only when the sociological and intellectual situation of Christianity had become radically insecure would relatively far-fetched and paranormal lines in apologetics begin to appear attractive.

Even before Mansel, however, change was already under way. Romantic poets using psychotropic drugs showed just the combination of attitudes that I have described, for they regarded abnormal mental states as being specially bardic and inspired, and at the same time they wished to become the fascinated spectators of their own inner histories.

Serious interest in mysticism began soon afterwards. We find Schopenhauer speaking highly of Eastern and Western mystics in a modern tone of voice – the first philosopher so to speak since late-classical times. J. Görres (*Christian Mysticism*, 1836–42) wrote the first scholarly study, and L. A. Feuerbach (*The Essence of Christianity*, 1841) brilliantly exploited mystical texts in developing his radical philosophy of religion.

Yet in spite of this auspicious beginning, interest still grew only very slowly, and it was not until the century's end that the trickle of books grew to a flood. Alongside William James and Jung, writers such as W. R. Inge, Henri Bremond, F. von Hügel and Evelyn Underhill became well known. Rudolf Otto, Martin Buber and others produced philosophies of religious experience, and many others saw in mysticism the starting point for a new type of apologetics.

This was novel, but there were also novel difficulties. What was to be said to those old-fashioned folk who declared that although they had always believed and practised their religion they had never had any of these new-fangled 'experiences', and did not see why they should have them? There was an older tradition that strongly objected to the new emphasis on religious experience, declaring that it was not the aim of the religious life to gain such experiences for oneself, that their evidential value was minimal, and that mystics and ecstatics were commonly heterodox, pathological or pagan.

The enthusiasts for mystical experiences were caught in a bind. They wanted to argue from certain special experiences to the existence of God or, more modestly, to say that we should practise religion because doing so will help us to attain certain supremely valuable mystical states of consciousness. But their difficulty was and is that the phenomena to which they appeal have to be supernatural but not too abnormal; extraordinary enough to make some supernatural claims plausible, without being so odd as to be obviously freakish and pathological.

The trouble is that in the history of religions people have been quite undiscriminating. They have stopped at nothing in order to procure for themselves altered states of consciousness. They have seized upon and made use of any and every imaginable mind-bending device, and they have venerated every kind of insanity. To induce ecstasy people have resorted and still do resort to alcohol, marijuana, soma, tea-drinking, smoking, rythmic music and dancing, flagellation, vigils, fasting, *coitus reservatus*, yogic techniques, chewing laurel leaves and much else. Often nowadays the ecstasies sought and obtained by such means are purely secular, as in the world of popular entertainment.

As for involuntary ecstasies, people have been and still are very ready to describe in religious terms mental states that psychiatrists prefer to connect with migraine, epilepsy, parietal lobe brain damage, schizophrenia, out-of-the-body experiences and hallucinations.

Late in the twentieth century, all the old habits remain strong. As the chemical and drugs industries produce fresh psychotropic agents, there are always some people ready to seize upon them for religious purposes. And demagogues make use for their own ends of the knowledge that people are more suggestible in conditions of fatigue, darkness, flickering light and ranting.

Historically, then, it seems that people have always had an insatiable appetite for ecstatic experiences, and have been willing to seek them by virtually any means available. Those moderns, therefore, who have wished to claim that some mystical and religious experiences are authentic, cognitive perhaps, and certainly highly valuable, need criteria to sift the wheat from the chaff. It is impossible to endorse everything that people have done and are still prepared to do in order to obtain ecstasy, so we must find a criterion that will separate genuine religious experiences from those that are merely artificially induced or pathological parodies of the real thing.

But the required criterion cannot be found. There is no way in which what is genuine and religiously valuable can be cleanly separated from what is abnormal and involuntary, or has been induced by artificial and excessive means. Dostoevsky used to have visionary experiences while an epileptic fit was developing. He knew they were pathological, but he also regarded them as valuable and revelatory – and that is the way it is. As theologians put it, the divine always comes to us in frail earthen vessels. Revelation, whether scriptural or personal, is never presented to us quite pure, uncontaminated and unmistakable. And in the present case, the case of religious, mystical or extraordinary experience, how could any such experience be both stunningly remarkable from a religious point of view and yet at the same time be so obviously normal and natural as somehow to be immune from the threat of reductive explanation? If it is indeed odd, then it will invite explanation. If it has arisen involuntarily, then the explanation will doubtless be in terms of some kind of cerebral abnormality; if some technique has been used to induce it, then the physiologist will be able to set about explaining how the technique works to induce the experience. But there is no way of securing some, or indeed any, episode in our mental life against the threat of naturalistic explanation.

Enthusiasts for mysticism and religious experience have faced even greater difficulties over the question of experience and interpretation. It is easy to recognize that we bring our own beliefs and our current concerns to our experience, so that everybody has religious experiences that confirm beliefs he already holds, or at least has been revolving in his own mind. In each religious tradition, experience is shaped by doctrine. Yet, at the same time, mystics of different faiths seemed to have a good deal in common. The solution appeared to lie in making a distinction of the natural religion/positive religion type. The phenomena can be explained if we suppose that there is a universal 'perennial philosophy' to which mysticism all over the world bears witness, but to which each of the particular positive religions has added its own local over-beliefs.

Now the question arises of precisely how mystical experiences are supposed to show that the perennial philosophy is true. The philosopher W. T. Stace, in a classic study, listed what he saw as the leading characteristics of mystical experience, and a scale devised by him has been widely used by psychologists of religion. Slightly rephrased for clarification, it is as follows:

1. Unity
   (a) within the subject
   (b) of the world experienced

2. Transcendence of time and space

3. Deeply felt positive mood of
   (a) joy, blessedness and peace
   (b) love

4. Sacredness

5. Objectivity and reality

6. Paradoxicality

7. Ineffability

8. Transiency

9. Lasting, positive effects on the subject's attitudes and behaviour towards
   (a) himself
   (b) others
   (c) life in general
   (d) the experience itself.

The suggestion is then that mystical experience is everywhere found to possess some blend of these characteristics and that philosophers have elaborated on them to build up the perennial philosophy, which turns out to be a kind of monistic idealism somewhere between neo-platonism and the Vedanta.

So the story goes, and it is all the wrong way round, a mystification from start to finish. Because we are products of a tradition originally shaped by Plato, and because in the nineteenth century we were enormously impressed by the discovery of Indian religion and mysticism and the affinities between the Indian traditions in metaphysics and our own, and because in the same nineteenth century many intellectuals rejected Christian dogma in favour of Spinoza and pantheism and idealism – for all these historical and cultural reasons people have been led to believe in something they have called the perennial philosophy, and therefore they have characterized mysticism in such a way as to confirm their own predilections. Stace's 'nine dimensions of religious experience' are

THE MIRROR OF THE SOUL

themselves a cultural creation with a readily-traceable history, and are just as arbitrarily imposed upon experience by some, as are the categories of evangelical theology by others.

What is objectively *there* prior to any interpretation, if one may so speak, is nothing but a physiological state of the body. Culture alone gives it meaning, or (in the older idiom) makes it 'mental', makes it into experience. The physiological state is given meaning and significance for an individual person by a combination of the cultural milieu he inhabits, and the setting in his own life in which it occurs.

To say this is not to say anything seriously 'reductive', if that matters, for the experience as interpreted may still be of the very greatest moral and religious significance to the subject. Only, he should not suppose that its meaning could possibly be as it were pure supernatural *datum*, for such an idea makes no sense. There is no quite extra-cultural standpoint from which cultural values and meanings can be extrinsically validated. Such a standpoint is not available to us, and such validation is not necessary.

What then can it be that accounts for the similarities of mystical-experience reports from around the world? The answer is not far to seek. In the mystical experience our ordinary capacity to impose temporal succession upon experience breaks down, so that we have a feeling of successivelessness, or eternity. Our ordinary ability to discriminate segments of space breaks down, so that we have a feeling of spacelessness. Our ordinary ability to define outer and inner structures breaks down, so that we have a feeling of unity. Even the ability to distinguish between the inner and the outer worlds breaks down, so that we are led to suppose that we have overcome the subject-object distinction and are in a state of absolute knowledge.

Nor is this all. Usually anxiety, simple anxiety over our own survival and well-being, forces us to be scrupulous precisionists who order and categorize our world, and scan it for signs of trouble. But in the mystical experience we take a holiday from the pernickettiness of discriminating observation and discursive reason. Anxiety recedes: we no longer need to think in functional terms, nor to attempt to control experience by the use of language. Instead we are filled with a sense of ineffable sacredness, and a blissfully undifferentiated and anxiety-free consciousness.

So the mystical experience has a similar shape around the world because it has one common feature — in it, we are out of our normal wits. The grandiose metaphysical belief in a Higher World above and in the possibility of absolute and intuitive knowledge, which has haunted the whole history of European thought, was nothing but an illusion. It was a mere negative, the suspension of our ordinary will to impose order and to discriminate within the field of experience, which was first turned into a positive and then mythicized, reified and inflated – but was, in the end, a mere illusion.

I am not, however, suggesting that mystical and religious experiences are of no value. On the contrary, they are of very great value, provided that we do not mistake their nature or make false claims about them. William James was correct in suggesting that the complete relaxation of tension that one gets in contemplative experience is immensely valuable as a moral (and, I would add, as a cognitive) holiday.

Still more important, although there is no Higher Realm to be seen on the way out into the mystical experience, there is something highly significant to be seen on the way back from it into our normal cognition and form of consciousness. Having enjoyed our little spell of transcendence, during the re-entry phase we are able to see really clearly, and as if for the first time, what our ordinary experience of the world and our ordinary working consciousness really is. We learn the great truth that the magic world of religion is simply the world seen from the religious (that is, the re-entrant) point of view.

Incidentally, this account explains why in scripture the climax of a theophany or a christophany is the commissioning by which the experient is sent back with his vocation – into the common world.

PART III

A COMMON LIFE

I

The Heathen

Human beings are usually highly ethnocentric.[1] Society seems to implant in us an almost invincible confidence that our world-view, our beliefs, customs and values, are the best there could be, and that alternatives to them are abominations. It is only human nature that we should nevertheless be fascinated by travellers' tales of the odd goings-on among exotic foreign peoples (Herodotus, Marco Polo, Mandeville), but the fascination is tinged with a certain dread. Foreigners are ritually unclean and forbidden, and their strange ways are felt to be threatening.

In this connection we may well ask why there are so many different cultures. Why are there something like one thousand languages in Papua New Guinea, and how are we to account for the extraordinary radiation of man?

There is, of course, an evolutionary advantage in it, for their cultural diversification has enabled human beings to colonize and to survive in a greater variety of habitats than any other creature. Most cultures – including ones that insist most vehemently on the need to hold fast to tradition – are a good deal more fluid and rapidly changing than we usually realize. Thus in the early 1970s there took place out on the iced-over Bering Strait a very poignant meeting, when the Siberian and Alaskan Eskimos met each other for the first time in half a century. Eskimos attach immense importance to such contacts, but in this particular case they had long been separated by the wretched accident of finding themselves to be technically citizens of the USSR and USA respectively, and therefore forbidden to meet. The joy of the accidental encounter was intense, but it was immediately succeeded by grief and dismay. In only fifty years, their language had split and they could no longer understand each other. So the Siberians had to speak Russian and the Alaskans English, and a white man who happened to be present found himself acting as interpreter.

In political contexts this people are now commonly called the Inuit, but anthropologists still retain the older name of Eskimos. They were culturally Upper Palaeolithic, and are a very well-documented people because the ice preserves so much. Eskimo archaeology is a fast-growing subject. So in this particular case we can actually prove the point about the normality of rapid change. Because they lived a very hard life in small isolated groups it might be thought that the Eskimos were an ultra-conservative people, but it was not so at all. Since they spread over their present territories in medieval times they have been in continual change, and were already so before ever they met the white man. It was our own mythic ways of thinking that led us to fancy that a hunting people without writing or law, and without pottery or the techniques of working hot metal, must somehow be primeval and unchanging. Not a bit of it; and what is true of the Eskimos is true of many other peoples as well. They may lack historians, but they do not lack histories.

It could be said that the clue to the whole history of the social sciences, and to their unpopularity, is that they have demanded continual unlearning. To understand an alien culture we must give up a great many assumptions which not only are difficult to recognize and to part with, but which also have been very firmly instilled into us by our own society, and are regarded by it as being highly important. Modern social anthropology could only have developed in pluralistic, sceptical and fast-changing times when people thought that it might be possible to apply the methods of the natural sciences to the study of society. In earlier periods, sympathetic and accurate accounts of exotic belief were very rare. The few examples, such as Plutarch's account of the Isis and Osiris myths, themselves come from the sort of sceptical circles that we have described.

Certainly Christianity had no innate sympathy towards alien faiths. It was from the beginning highly aware of other religions, but vehemently hostile to them. It denounced them as superstitious and idolatrous, it attacked their myths as immoral, it described their rituals as satanic parodies of the Christian sacraments, and it used exorcism to drive out the residual influence of their divinities from the souls of catechumens. (On all these points, see Justin Martyr's *First Apology*.)

It is often said that Christianity took over pagan feasts and holy places; but in doing so it was in no way prompted by sympathy. The Venerable Bede (*Ecclesiastical History* 1, xxx) transcribes a letter from Pope Gregory I to the Abbot Mellitus, written in AD 601, which lays down the policy to be followed in Britain. In it the Pope describes the old gods as devils, but says that it is not possible to efface everything at once from the obdurate minds of the British. Instead the church must take over the old temples and rites and, so to say, *bury* the old religion by superimposing Christianity upon every bit of it, so that nothing recognizable of it can survive.

This classical attitude to other religions was to prove very tenacious. The view that they were idolatrous, based on fear and demon-ridden was still vigorous in the nineteenth century, and is frequently to be found even in the twentieth. But the voyages of exploration, and later the missionary movement, gradually increased knowledge of other cultures. One can, for example, find friendly observations about Islam in Locke, about Confucianism in Leibniz and about Hinduism in Toland.

Attitudes were however often ambiguous. The tendency to idealization is illustrated by Dryden's 'Conquest of Granada':

> I am as free as Nature first made man,
> Ere the base laws of servitude began,
> When wild in woods the noble savage ran.

There was certainly a strong desire in many quarters to believe in the natural human being and in natural religion. Actual examples, however, seemed not to be forthcoming. On the contrary, human nature and religion seemed everywhere to be just as 'positive' or conventional, and as superstitious, as the Christianity that the intellectual *avant-garde* was turning away from. So on the rebound people could fly to the opposite attitude, as exemplified by Pope:

> Lo the poor Indian! whose untutor'd mind
> Sees God in clouds or hears him in the wind;
> His soul proud science never taught to stray
> Far as the solar walk or milky way. . . . [2]

The ablest early book on comparative religion was probably David Hume's *The Natural History of Religion* (1757).[3] Crude though it is by later standards, its chief theses are still worth recalling.

Hume separates the question of the origin of religious belief from its grounds. It was clear to him that the first human beings could not have been philosophical reasoners who used the argument from design to arrive at belief in a wise, good and benevolent Creator. On the contrary, his reading of Herodotus, Livy and the Old Testament suggested to Hume that in the earliest times the gods had been many and capricious. It was inexplicable misfortune, the changes and chances of life and its unknown terrors, which had first set men a-sacrificing and a-praying. Early human beings did not see the world as orderly and beautiful, but as a theatre of conflicting, terrible and unpredictable powers that they needed to propitiate.

In the mood of Hobbes, Hume thus seeks a genetic explanation of the origin of religion in terms of the emotions and the life-situation of early human beings: but he forgets the impossibility of testing such an explanation. In fact, we know nothing of the psychology of the earliest people.

Secondly, Hume argues that religion is not 'natural' or innate, but is a human construction. As an empiricist, he accepts no innate ideas. Like ethics, religion must therefore be explained anthropocentrically, in terms of the mind's response to the impact of the environment upon it. Here Hume shows himself the forerunner of later projection-theories of religion and morality.

Hume is again close to Hobbes in being an emotivist: religious belief represents an expressive or emotive response to the perceived human situation. The origin of religion, as he puts it, is in the passions and not the reason.

Fourthly and finally, Hume argues that polytheism came before monotheism. For a moment he joins the Whigs in rejecting the idea of a primitive Golden Age and instead arguing that there has been an ascent of man from lower to higher, from barbarism to civilization, and from polytheism to monotheism. But being a sceptical, ironical man and also a Tory, Hume then teasingly argues for the superiority of polytheism.

One further eighteenth-century idea deserves a passing mention. In 1760 Charles de Brosses' *Du culte des dieux fetiches* introduced the term 'fetishism' as a general characterization of the religion of preliterate man. The word lasted for over a century, helping to fix the prejudice that other people are idolaters, and was to be adapted to new polemical uses by the Marxists and by Freud.

All this, however, has been mere background. With the nineteenth century a whole flood of new interests and influences arrived which were to open up entirely new possibilities. The growth of the colonial empires and of missionary activity brought a great increase in the volume of reports reaching Europe about other cultures. At the same time within Europe the Romantic Movement had overthrown the rationalism of the preceding age, enabling people to look with new eyes at many neglected areas of life. Thus the rise of nationalism created an interest in folklore, folksong, folkdancing, folk art and peasant culture generally as expressive of the spirit of the people. Something very new, an *aesthetic interest in religion*, appeared.[4] At the same time with the widespread loss of faith there arose an anxiety, even a compulsive need, to explain what religion had been and why, in modern times, it had at last been outgrown.

Given this background it is not surprising that the first scientific interpretations of religion commonly saw it as having belonged to the childhood of the race, and as involving what now appeared to be serious intellectual errors.

2

Spirit Beings

In his books on fundamentalism and how to escape from it, James Barr asks what philosophical position underlies the conservative evangelical protestantism so rife nowadays around the English-speaking world. The twice-born are not exactly reflective people, but Barr reports that some of their nineteenth-century American precursors acknowledged the influence of the old Scottish Common-sense philosophy. He argues that so far as Evangelicals can be said to have a philosophy, they do indeed still stand in that tradition.

Barr is right, and his thesis surely applies not only to the evangelicals but also to liberals and to large sections of the general public in the English-speaking countries, where the influence of the fathers of modern thought, Kant and Hegel, has still not yet penetrated deeply. A kind of naïve realism prevails, and it leads to a very realist and doctrinal view of religion.

All this was particularly true for the early anthropologists and the cultural background from which they mostly emerged. For many ordinary people in the early nineteenth century religious belief provided what still seemed a pretty complete theory of the world, and it dominated the personality of the believer. His stocks of historical and scientific knowledge and his professional and other life-skills were not yet so vigorous and bulky as to threaten the overriding authority of religious belief at the very centre of his life and personality. And he understood his religious beliefs in what can only be called a strongly factual way.

It needs to be emphasized that a realist or 'intellectualist' theory of what religious beliefs are supposed to mean was, and very often still is, taken for granted by unbelievers even more than by believers. We can summarize it as follows: the practice of religion presupposes the holding of religious beliefs, religious beliefs are explanatory hypotheses that purport to account for things, and religion differs from science in that whereas science explains things in terms of the operation of impersonal forces, mathematical rules etc., religion explains things in terms of the activity of invisible spirit beings. Religion was rather similar to science, except that it invoked the activity of unseen persons, whereas science invokes physical law.

The great nineteenth-century anthropologists were usually lapsed protestants, and most of them held the theory of the meaning of religious beliefs that I have just described. Writing about 'primitive man', they were in many ways writing about their own childhood and about the faith that they themselves had outgrown. So they set out to show how primitives, lacking the scientific method and tending always to personify whatever they were dealing with, made childlike mistakes in reasoning and became trapped in factually false beliefs. These errors have only gradually been shaken off with the progress of civilization.

It is already obvious that this theory of religion was useful at various levels. On the largest scale it could be invoked to justify imperial protection of the more childlike and backward races of mankind, and on the smallest scale it was a disguised apologia for the anthropologist's own personal position. In addition, it was amplified by a number of supporting myths. The early social scientists were broadly evolutionary, progressive and Whig in outlook. They believed in stages of civilization, in higher and lower races and in laws of historical development. So they pictured cultural evolution as passing through a standard series of steps in the course of the great ascent from Them to Us. Laws of historical change prescribed the development from savagery to barbarism to civilization; from animism to religion, to philosophy and on to science; from primitive promiscuity to group marriage, to polygamy, to monogamy; from community of goods to private property; and finally, from external and materialistic religion to internalized, spiritual religion and so on to humanism.

In one thinker after another we notice the influence of these and similar developmental models. The presumption is that the history of the race has been a steady onward and upward movement from Them to Us, so we may suppose that they began at the furthest remove from us, and have evolved step by step towards what we now are.

All these ideas were already present in the founder of sociology, Auguste Comte (1798–1857), author of the *Cours de la philosophie positive* (1830–42). Comte held that human nature is always and everywhere basically the same and follows, at varying rates, the same course of development. A Baconian method is therefore adequate for social science: we simply collect the facts about all known societies, and then arrange them in order of improvement. The sequence thus constructed will show us from present evidence the course of all mankind's cultural evolution.

Furthermore, Comte saw that there are significant correlations between the different classes of social fact, economic, legal, religious and so on. Map all these correlations, work out the connections, and you will have a comprehensive empirical sociology.

The main stages in the evolution of culture were the theological, the metaphysical and the 'positive' or scientific. The first era, in which religious thought is dominant, was further subdivided by Comte into three stages: Fetishism, Polytheism and Monotheism.

All this may suggest that Comte was strongly post-religious in outlook. This is not so. He believed that the human race was evolving into a single community, a Church of Man, in which humanity itself would be the supreme object of veneration. He thus reached the same kind of radical humanist religious position as Feuerbach, but independently and from a different starting-point, for Comte's background was Saint-Simonian, whereas Feuerbach's was Hegelian. Both claimed to be still religious thinkers, but Comte was the more effective in practice, being the founder of the rich and ornate humanist religion of Positivism.

Nowadays it is customary to mock Comte. We may forget that the noble dream of a universal Church of Humanity, blending the moral values of Jesus with those of socialist humanism, remained highly attractive to many people at least until the time of the First World War.

Herbert Spencer (1820–93), author of the *Principles of Sociology* (1877), was also a sort of Feuerbachian who turned from God to man, from theology to anthropology, but his argument for doing so was different again. He appealed to Kant, as interpreted by Sir William Hamilton and H. L. Mansel, to justify his agnosticism about metaphysical and religious questions and his consequent turning to science and the realm of the knowable.

In his theory of religion Spencer was a Euhemerist. Like many of his contemporaries he believed that dreams, shadows and reflections had given rise to the belief in an immaterial soul or ghost that could exist apart from the body. This led to the veneration of the ghosts of ancestors, which in turn developed into the belief in gods.

Interestingly, there is one overtly Euhemerist nineteenth-century religion, Mormonism. But in general Spencer's theory of the origin of religious belief suffers from the usual disadvantages of having no evidence in its favour, and being untestable. There are of course some religions, such as that of ancient Egypt, and especially Taoism, in which outstanding human beings have regularly been promoted to divine status; but there is no reason to think that all gods began life as human beings.

E. B. (Sir Edward) Tylor (1832–1917), is a more substantial figure, and his *Primitive Culture* (1871; second edition, 1873) is often regarded as the founding text of social anthropology. His great book is highly typical of its period not only in the ways we have already described but also in its darwinism and in the prominence it gives to the problem of religion.

Tylor introduced 'culture' as the proper subject matter of social anthropology, defining it as the common ways of whole peoples. Announcing his programme as 'a natural history of society', Tylor describes seven different relations that there may be between the cultural present and its past: progression, degradation, survival, revival, diffusion, modification and permanence. Most of these have close parallels in biology. For example, a case of cultural survival might be the non-functional cuff-buttons, lapels and slits in my jacket, which bear witness to its military and sporting ancestry. They may be compared with vestigial organs in biology, such as the appendix in my belly, which were once functional but are so no longer. Degradation in culture, such as happened with the Tasmanians and some Pacific peoples, is analogous to the simplification of the bodies of parasitic and troglodytic animals. Cultural permanence is comparable with the sharks and the king-crabs (= horseshoe crabs), who having a good design in a stable environment have simply stayed around.

Revival was an oddity. By it Tylor was drawing attention to the curious recrudescence of very ancient beliefs that may occur in advanced industrial societies, as when shamanism reappears in the guise of spiritualism. Tylor was a firm believer in progress and in the analogy, as children to adults, so savages are to us. The modern revival of belief in spirits (and astrology, and witchcraft, and much else) was decidedly embarrassing to him.

One possible solution was to extend the child-adult metaphor to the relations of the social classes, on the (rather large) assumption that the upper and more educated classes are indeed more 'advanced' and less superstitious than the lower. Tylor does indeed use much the same 'social arithmetic', the Bacon-and-Darwin method of reconstructing historical development from present phenomena, as Comte. We can be sure, he thinks, that the lower races — and perhaps also the lower classes — have developed less far than the higher. And survivals give us additional grounds for confidence that reliable evidence of the past is to be found among present phenomena.

Are there laws in sociology, in some sense strong enough to rule out human freedom? Tylor professes himself agnostic on the point. Much of human behaviour obviously does have causes, and it is sufficient for the social scientist to say that he proposes to investigate human behaviour so far as it is caused and to see how far his enquiry takes him.

Tylor's realism shows in the way he defines religion not as activity or institution or symbol-system, but simply as creed: 'the belief in Spiritual Beings'. The belief is for Tylor mistaken and illusory, but it is nonetheless factual. That he does see religious beliefs as erroneous factual beliefs shows very clearly in his celebrated discussion of why people go on believing that magic works. Reading between the lines, it is clear that Tylor has in mind not merely magic in the narrow sense, but all ritual action, including the sacraments and prayers of modern Christians.

Consider now the form of Tylor's discussion, and the questions he raises and answers. He asks, why do people perform magical and religious actions? Answer: because they think that there are gods and spirits with influence over human well-being, and that the actions when properly performed will affect the weather, the crops, illness and so on.

How did such beliefs first arise? From the need to understand and control the natural world. And why do people accept them? Because they have grown up in a culture in which such beliefs are received and socially-legitimated truths.

But — and here is the crucial question — why do people go on believing in such things in spite of the testimony of experience? Tylor replies that there are many reasons why people cling to non-rational

beliefs. It is human nature to pay far more attention to the one case
where the magic has seemed to work than to the many cases where it
has failed. In some cases, as in magic to make the sun rise or rain fall,
the event was perhaps going to occur anyway. Magic may depend on
trickery, or be combined with craft-skills that really do work.
Predictions may be couched in very vague terms, or be in some way
self-fulfilling. The failure of magic can always be ascribed to
improper performance of the ritual, or to the presence of counter-
magic.

Summing up, Tylor says that factors such as these act as blocks to
falsification and are all the more effective in a traditional society
which lacks the experimental method. His whole discussion is
thoroughly positivist in tone. He assumes that religious beliefs do
make factual claims that are promptly falsified by any strict
application of scientific tests; and then he gives reasons why people
do not in fact renounce these erroneous beliefs as they should.

It cannot be denied that there are superstitious believers of whom
Tylor's analysis is true. Not long ago a certain well-known religious
figure found he had cancer. He treated the event as a test of his faith
and declared publicly that he would pray for a cure. It goes without
saying that he died, that his 'faith' was therefore falsified, and that
the obituaries, the commentators in the church press and his many
thousands of followers laboured mightily – and entirely effectively –
to conceal the truth from themselves.

Thus far, Tylor is right; but those of whom he is right are,
precisely, the superstitious – those who attribute an occult quasi-
technical efficacy to religious action. And non-superstitious people
do not do this.

I am about to attend a family wedding. Why do we go? To rally
round, to witness and to legitimate the couple's union and give them
encouragement, support, good wishes and a good send-off, and to
celebrate marriage itself, the family and our kinship as being among
life's chief sources of happiness. No occult causality is involved, only
value-affirming and life-structuring symbolic action. When I pray for
the sick, am I applying and testing a special therapeutic technique?
Of course not, for something far more important than that is
involved. In praying urgently for one who is sick, we express loving
concern for and sympathetic self-identification with a fellow human
in distress. So long as that particular value is maintained in our
common life, just so long will human life continue to be worth living.

The affirmation of our values is a far greater and more important thing than the application of techniques.

Tylor's great distinction as an anthropologist was recognized when he was appointed to a Readership in the subject at Oxford in 1884, the world's first academic post in Anthropology. His Comtist and intellectualist view of religion was continued by J. G. (Sir James) Frazer (1854–1941), but Frazer's celebrated *Golden Bough* (1890–1915) is not of great theoretical interest, except in its treatment of the relations of magic, science and religion.

According to Frazer the earliest human world view was magical. The first human beings needed to understand and, still more, to control their environment, and magic represents their first attempt to do this. Like natural science, magic expresses the confidence that the world is law-governed and controllable by man.

Unhappily the confidence proved unjustified and magic was found not to work. The next step in the argument recalls the young Hegel's account of Noah in *The Spirit of Christianity and its Fate*,[5] for Frazer says that when early man saw that he did not have enough power to solve his own problems for himself, he fell under the illusion that his only way of getting help was to become the servant of spirits whom he believed to possess the power over nature that he needed. Religion thus represents an indirect and rather 'feminine' attempt to gain power through self-subjection.

However, the abler people realized in due course that the belief in spirits or gods was also vain, and so the second great transition occurred, from religion to science.

Frazer's theory is so redolent of the scientism of its period that it is something of a surprise to learn that he was privately a timorously agnostic Christian. By his time the intellectualist view of the nature of religious beliefs was reaching such a pitch of absurdity that one can only say that he and others like him had entirely lost their grip on what the word 'god' means and how it functions in the religious life.

In any case, his theory has everything wrong with it. The idea of three successive stages, magic, religion and science, is wholly unsupported by the evidence. Even among the simplest hunter-gatherers very high-class observation and techniques can be found; and even in an advanced civilization magic persists and is often interwoven with an advanced technology, as in the making of a Japanese sword. Belief in gods and spirits is to be found in virtually every society, simple or complex, ancient or modern. Finally, magic is not technical and concerned with nature, but is very strongly traditional, social and expressive.

By the end of the nineteenth century the severe limitations of a realist or intellectualist interpretation of religion were becoming apparent. It leaves too much out. On the realist view it is hard to see how more than one at most of the thousands of religions can be substantially true, and perhaps a few others partially so. The bulk of the whole religious life of mankind has to be regarded as having been simply a mistake, an error, an illusion. But if so, why has religion always been so important in every society?

Yet in spite of all this, so large a proportion of ordinary religious believers still remain themselves theological realists that we who argue against realism find ourselves in a tiny minority. A symbolist-expressive view of religion may have become normal among those who study religion objectively, but it is not yet customary among the believers themselves. Part of the reason must be that the majority of believers still think and act most of the time as if there is only one religion in the world that deserves serious consideration. A social scientist cannot take such a view.

3

Making Good

Towards the end of the nineteenth century, we have been suggesting, a complex shift in religious thought began to take place.

In part, it was a reaction against the evolutionism of Tylor and other senior figures. In *The Making of Religion* (1898), the gifted Scottish amateur Andrew Lang had a chapter titled 'High Gods of Low Races', arguing that something approximating to monotheism is reported among peoples of very simple technology. Lang and such later writers as W. Schmidt were even to have some success in reviving the idea of primitive monotheism.

At the same time there began a movement from an intellectualist to an emotivist view of religion.[6] Bertrand Russell's distinction between logic and mysticism (later to be adopted and amended by Wittgenstein) was a distinction between a scientific-rationalist and an affective response to the world. Simply by making the distinction Russell was rejecting the idea that religion is no more than a kind of primitive animistic science, chiefly concerned with cognition and explanation. A religious response to the world is different in kind from the scientific attitude, and has its own distinctive place in our lives.

In the same period, the 1890s, Lang suggested that the origin of religion should be traced to 'an unanalysable *sensus numinis*', and R. R. Marett (1866–1943) was undercutting Tylor by describing a 'pre-animistic' stage of religious thought. In this early condition of thought magic and religion were not yet clearly distinct, so Marett used the term 'magico-religious' to describe it. He took up the word *mana* from Melanesia to describe the impersonal sacred power which may charge certain persons, things and places. *Mana*, he suggested, was the original religious object.

Marett was probably wrong about *mana*, and his emotivism is in any case better illustrated by his treatment of magic and other rituals. We should attend less, he says, to what savages think or are supposed to think, and more to what they feel and what they do. Accordingly he treats magic as a displacement-activity or a symbolic substitute-activity, like shaking your fist at somebody instead of punching his nose. In such a case I perform, not the act itself, but a ritualized substitute for it. 'Primitive religion', says Marett, 'is something not so much thought out as danced out'. He emphasizes that the content of primitive religion consists entirely of traditionally-prescribed behaviour – custom. Of the savage he says memorably that 'Between him and the unknown stands nothing but his custom'.

In a similar vein, William Robertson Smith (1846–1894) also reacted against the individualism and the intellectualism of Tylor's approach to religion. Smith shifts the emphasis to society: 'Religion in primitive times was not a system of belief with practical applications: it was a body of fixed traditional practices, to which every member of society conformed as a matter of course.'

We will look at sociological theories of religion in the next chapter: for the present we will pursue the theme of psychological expressivism or emotivism. It is important because emotivism, in religion as in ethics, has a bad name and we need to change the way we see it.

In ethics, emotivism is commonly taken to be the doctrine that our moral judgments are mere expressions of subjective feeling. They evince personal likes and dislikes which we certainly seek to persuade others to share, but which in fact have no more objective and rational basis than a personal like or dislike for a food-flavour. Similarly, religious emotivism is the doctrine that religious faith and activity have no cognitive content but serve merely to express our feelings. Thus understood, emotivism has a bad name, for it sounds like a disparaging and reductive theory, such as might be held by a positivist philosopher who finds morality and religion to be boring subjects and makes a few dismissive remarks about their lack of intellectual content before moving on to something more interesting.

This account suggests that emotivism has got its bad name from its relation to the metaphysics of positivism. I mean that the positivists were people who held that there is no testable objective knowledge in morality or religion, that through natural science we do gain objective knowledge of the world of fact, and that philosophy should be interested only in objective knowledge. The positivists were typical realists in the way they virtually equated rationality with objectivity. Emotivism was a way of saying that in losing their objective cognitive content morality and religion had come down in the world. They now compared very unfavourably with natural science, and had ceased to be of interest to thinkers.

That is the impression of emotivism that people still have. It is a mistake, as the case of David Hume shows. Hume had thought it possible to secure natural science and our ordinary empirical knowledge while being cheerfully sceptical about metaphysics, religion and ethics – but it was not, and he ended in general scepticism. Similarly, in modern times, the positivism which thought that the world of fact would stand firm after metaphysics, religion and ethics had been demoted has itself run into difficulties.

Today, after factual and scientific knowledge have lost their relatively privileged status, they are no longer able to make everything else seem second best compared with themselves. We can look again at ethical emotivism, and we now see that in fact it was like Sartre's existentialist ethics. It was a form of voluntarism, and it emphasized human creativity. It was a way of saying that we ourselves are the only source of the values we live by. We do it all: it is all up to us. Now we see that the move in religious thought at the very beginning of this century towards action, emotion and expression was highly significant. It was the arrival of the post-Nietzschean age. People were beginning to grasp that apart from us and what we do there is no moral order, nor any other kind of order in the world. Existence is everlastingly meaningless, chaotic and futile. It is only by a supreme effort of human creativity, imposing order, meaning and value upon the 'white noise' of existence, that life is made possible. A people's religion is that stock of traditional structures of order, symbolic meaning and value by which their existence as a people with a way of life and an identity is constituted. Hence Marett's saying that between the savage and the unknown stands nothing but his custom, a saying that gives one the *frisson* that is the mark of quality. Culture is the Dance of Death.

These reflections have changed our valuations, for we now see that the most important human beings of all are the makers of meaning and value – the artists, the moral innovators and, above all, the religiously creative. For our religions are purely human creations that in most cases have slowly evolved in a practical, trial-and-error, emotive, collective and unconscious way over a long period. They are our own inventions – but so is everything else, including even we ourselves – and they are the most important of all our creations, for they embody the fundamental moral structures of existence that constitute us as persons and gives us our identity.

In the light of this we can now seek a new way of describing the psychological-expressivist or emotivist strain in religious thought that emerged around 1900.

The new suggestion was that instead of being bad or primitive science, religion is not in fact in the same business as science at all. Like a dance, it expresses an affective response to the world. Expression and practice are prior to theory and speculation. They are older and more fundamental.

That being so, we reverse the order of theory and practice. Religion begins as ritual, symbolic action expressing social values and acting as the vehicle for cosmic feelings of dread, neediness, gratitude, guilt or whatever. Around the rituals, stories develop. They are myths, which postulate sources for the values and objects of the feelings. Later, speculative thought attempts to rationalize the myths.

In this way practice and unconscious collective feeling come to be thought of as prior to belief and as determining it. It is true that the myths and speculations that grow up are often aetiological: they look like attempts to explain the origin of the rituals and to justify the performance of them. But this is not to be taken too seriously, because the search for explanations is not in fact so important in religion as the intellectualists used to suppose.

Emotivism has often been associated with a projection theory of religion, and since projection theories were typical of such celebrated unbelievers as Feuerbach, Marx, Freud and Durkheim, they have tended to give emotivism a bad name. But once again, this is a mistake. We can reformulate the science-religion contrast so as to show why.

The realism of science and its value-neutrality are two faces of the same coin. Science projects out the world as inert, mind-independent, objectified raw material. The aim is to understand the properties and behaviour of this material, with a view to gaining technical control over it. But by constituting its own subject-matter in these terms science inevitably has a chronic problem with values. Hence our modern *anomie*.

By contrast, religion tackles reality practically, seeking to make a world that will satisfy the heart, fulfil our desires and be a home for us. It seeks to humanize the world by imposing upon it symbols that represent the ideal, the as-yet-unattained, the heart's desire. Religion is our project for an ideal human community in a fully familiarized world.

Because science creates an inert, objectified and value-neutral world, it naturally sees religion as being anthropomorphic, emotive, expressive and a projection of human desires. And it is right, for religion is indeed all these things – and all the better for being so. For religion is total where science is partial. Religion does not deal with the world as it looks to an abstract mathematical intelligence, but with the world of man as an emotional, embodied, active social being.

Thus when we understand that religion is simply human we have not abolished it but have begun to grasp its true import. Human beings fulfil themselves by projecting and enacting their desires symbolically. So our highest spiritual self-realization is most effectively attained by projecting out the God-ideal, aspiring after God, ritually enacting our drawing-nigh to God and mystically attaining union with him. That is how we work, and the fact that with Feuerbach Western man at last became fully aware of how religion works ought not to betoken the end of religion but, rather, a quantum-leap forward in our religious life.

To do him justice, Ludwig Feuerbach (1804–1872) himself claimed to be a religious thinker. The unanimous verdict of Christians has been that *The Essence of Christianity* (1841) is one of the great works of unbelief, 'the thorn in the flesh of modern theology', as Karl Barth put it. But that view of Feuerbach is an injustice.

Feuerbach began as a theology student, and was deeply influenced by Hegel at Berlin. There were already some elements of projectionism in Hegel himself – the dominance of subjectivity, and the conception of religion as *Vorstellung* – but of course Feuerbach became a much more thoroughgoing projectionist. For him a religious object just is some element within human experience or human nature projected out, reified and made an object of worship. Following Hegel, Feuerbach says that whereas the objects of metaphysics take an abstract conceptual form, religious thought sees its objects in sensuous and imaginative terms.

Why the projection? Feuerbach holds that religion springs from a feeling of want, and that religious beliefs express disguised wishes. These wishes reflect our human helplessness, ignorance, unfreedom and inability to attain personal fulfilment. The religious object represents the imagined fulfilment of our wants, projected out, made into a real being, worshipped and aspired after in order that we may attain it.

At this point things may go either of two ways. Provided that we are fully conscious that our god is our own ultimate aim, our goal in life, and provided that religion actually works to achieve human spiritual emancipation, then Feuerbach is all in favour of it. For religion is about the descent of God into man: through religion God becomes man and man thereby becomes himself. Feuerbach's vision is of an integral divine humanism of self-giving love.

Unfortunately, however, things can go another way. The human mind has an inveterate tendency to fetishism: that is, we tend to project out, to make real beings of, and then to fall under the domination of, the creations of our own desires. If God ceases to be just my own god and becomes an objective and repressive being over against me, then instead of being an image of and a pathway to my salvation, he becomes a kind of tyrant and an obstacle to my self-realization.

Thus for Feuerbach the question about religion is whether it is so working as to keep people alienated and ignorant of what they can become, or whether it is so working as to bring about the full humanization of man.

Few of the well-known religious emotivists reach Feuerbach's level of insight, or make significant additions to the ideas we have already presented. Freud, as we saw earlier, recognized only the most alienated and fetishistic form of religion – in which respect, it must be confessed, some Christians resemble him. Rudolf Otto (1869–1937), though a very influential figure, does not add much theoretically to what may be found in Lang and Marett. Bronislaw Malinowski (1884–1942) thought of himself as a follower of Frazer, and is best remembered as the master of fieldwork method: but there are some interesting elements of emotivism in his ideas. He develops

Marett's account of magic, and he points to the way in which at funerals the community rallies round to reconstitute itself, reaffirm its solidarity and celebrate its values. These ideas, however, are interwoven with more sociological and functionalist themes, to which we now turn.

4

The Politics of Heaven

The late nineteenth century was a time when many new professions and branches of knowledge were struggling for recognition. Darwin's great success in giving biology a unifying theory and its own distinctive ways of thinking naturally provoked a great deal of envy. What he had achieved for his branch of science was precisely what many others were striving for in theirs. Inevitably there was some borrowing of his ideas, not least by social scientists.

The suggestion therefore began to be made that a human society can be compared with a biological organism; perhaps with some colonial organism or super-individual such as a sponge, a Portuguese man o' war (*Vellela*), or an ant colony. Darwin had taught us to read almost every detail of an animal's anatomy, physiology and behaviour as having some relevance to its survival and its passing-on of its genes; so perhaps the structure, the beliefs and the behaviour of the social organism might be interpreted in a similarly practical and functional way? The analogy suggests that religious beliefs and institutions would not be so universal unless they contributed significantly to society's survival and flourishing.[7]

We should not assume that this functionalist approach is in any objectionable sense reductive. It could be seen as pointing in the opposite direction. Where Tylor and other intellectualists had pictured virtually all societies everywhere before modern times as having been the captives of false beliefs, the functionalist was able to take a more generous view. If their basic beliefs were no more than simple errors, how had they been able to flourish? The religious beliefs of tribal and early civilized people must surely have had some adaptive significance, or have performed some valuable social function. And what was this function? The most potent theory has been that religion is the cement of society: that it symbolically represents the social order and works to maintain our allegiance to society and our acceptance of social authority.

When they first meet this theory in a strong form people usually react sceptically. They see that it might apply to a small-scale monocultural tribal religion, because in that kind of society religion and culture almost coincide. But the great multicultural scriptural religions exalt the prophet, the martyr and other rebels. There is often a clear distinction between the spheres of church and state, religion and culture. In large-scale pluralist societies many aspects of the social order are not represented in religion, and many things important in religion find little or no public and social expression.

Besides, people protest, the strong Durkheimian theory that God is society, or a personification of social authority, is mythical. Society is not a substance, nor an individual being with a mind of its own. 'Society' is just a word for the sum of all of the rules governing social behaviour, rules that have been slowly evolved by individuals through their common life together. These rules are staggeringly rich and complex, for they include all the rules governing language and manners and morals and religion and law and politics and economics and much else besides. But still, all we talk about when we talk about 'society' is a lot of rules, and no more. Society is not literally a being: literally, it is just a set of rules.

The critics are right to say that we do not nowadays find many all-out theocratic states of the sort in which religion is the prime bond of social unity and tool of social control. The new Islamic Republics may fit Durkheim's theory neatly, but they are very exceptional. However, within our loose-knit modern societies there are a great many subgroups, racial, ethnic and religious. Within these groups there are many people whose ethnic and cultural identity matters a great deal to them, and it is a matter of fact that that particular kind of 'identity' is still usually vested in religion. The system by which in the East the Archbishop was recognized as the Ethnarch was not arbitrary. We have long spoken of the Egyptian gods, the Greek gods, the Norse gods and the Hindu gods, as if those divinities embodied the national spirit of those peoples; but the fusion of religion with nationalism is by no means confined to the ancient polytheistic religions. It is a modern commonplace. And from the idioms people use it can sound very much as if, for example, among the Jews returning to God means the same as returning to Jewishness, and being faithful to God means the same as being faithful to one's own Jewishness.

There is thus rather more plausibility in sociological theories of religion than may appear at first sight, but for the sake of clarity it is worth distinguishing four different claims. I will call them borrowing, reinforcement, expression and reference.

The most modest claim is simply that religious language *borrows* metaphors from the social order, and it is obviously true. God is described as Father, King, Judge, Lord and so on. Although obvious, this fact of borrowing is highly significant, for it suggests that we might be able to write the early history of religious thought through the gradual becoming-available of the requisite metaphors. Thus, if it is essential to the idea of a god that he or she controls nature, then presumably people could not have believed in gods until their experience was supplying them with the necessary imagery of power and control over nature. They would need first to have experience of human kings, lords, judges and shepherds before they could transfer these terms to God.

The second claim is that religious action and belief in fact so function as to maintain and *reinforce* the authority of the social order, although it is not claimed that the connection is any more than contingent. By borrowing such metaphors as king, judge and lord religion naturally tends to hallow those institutions; and by the very order and regularity of its rites and its inculcation of virtue, religion commonly tends to pacify. Yet although this is evidently true, these effects of religion may be merely coincidental, and we need not conclude that they betray the real import of religious belief. For all I know, it may be that the piety and ethics of Methodism do tend to produce good shopkeepers, foremen or trades union officials, but it need not follow that the production of such people was in any sense whatever John Wesley's 'real' purpose. The reinforcement thesis merely points out a connection, without going so far as to claim that its effects in the social and political realm are the only criterion of the true meaning of religious belief.

The third claim is that ritual action gives symbolic *expression* to the social order; and it is a stronger claim, because it is now being

said that the social effects of religion are by no means merely
contingent. Correctly interpreted, the symbolism of religious rituals
unmistakably represents the social order and so functions as to
consolidate society and to confirm its values and its authority. The
sacralizing and validating effect of religion is not a mere coincidence, but is demonstrably built-in. For the present the only comment we will make on this thesis is that there are some sorts of
religion of which it seems to be true, and others of which it seems to
be untrue.

Finally, the last claim is the boldest. It is that religion is a set of
symbolic actions and beliefs, the true *referents* of which are to be
found in the social order. This thesis is explicitly reductive, in that a
believer who came to accept it would surely give up the practice of
religion (though note that, if a reductive explanation is the best
available explanation, then there can be nothing wrong with its
being reductive).

However, the gap between the believer's own self-understanding
and the observer's interpretation of him is a tricky point in
anthropology, and tricky for me. Many Christians think of God as
a really-existing invisible Person. I say that God is a personal
religious ideal, internal to the spiritual life. Many Christians appear
to regard my account as reductive. They think that they themselves
could only come to adopt my view at the price of losing their own
faith, and therefore that I ought to admit that I have lost mine. But I
deny this, pointing out that for me all of religious language is still
usable and the religious life is still livable. Moreover, the God-
ideal on my view remains transcendent, authoritative and irreduc-
ible, for, after all, I do not resolve the idea of God into non-religious
terms. So I say I believe in the true God, whereas the God of the
realists is an idol – all of which goes to show that whether or not a
particular theory of religion is reductionist, and whether or not you
can hold it and still be a believer, is often controversial and difficult
to decide.

A view of God such as mine may seem very individualistic and
'spiritual'. The key founders of the sociological interpretation of
religion began from the assumption that the most primitive type of
religion must have stood at the very opposite extreme, being highly
collective and materialistic. Robertson Smith, the author of *The
Religion of the Semites* (1889), thought that the earliest religions
had no dogmas, and lacked even myths; they consisted solely of

institutions and rites. But of all religious rites the most important and universal is sacrifice, and therefore a correct interpretation of sacrifice will provide the key to the whole theory of religion.

Robertson Smith believed – partly on philological grounds – that the earliest Semitic societies were composed of matrilineal clans, each of which was tied to a totem animal. The clansmen were of one blood with the totem and with each other, and the totem animal was seen as being the founder and spirit-father of the entire clan. Periodically the clansmen used to express their union with each other in the totem by slaying the totem animal and having a communion feast of its raw flesh. Out of this primal type of totemic communion-sacrifice the animal sacrifices of the Old Testament had later developed.

The crucial point about Robertson Smith's theory is that the most ancient type of religious object, the totem, symbolized the group; and the most important type of religious ritual, sacrifice, was a symbolic enactment and confirmation of group solidarity. Although there is now little doubt that Robertson Smith and those who followed him were wrong about totemism and very one-sided about sacrifice, it is not so obvious that they were wrong about the overwhelming and primal religious importance of our sociality. As the case of the *enfant sauvage* reminds us, we human beings cannot become human – because we cannot become rational, because we cannot become language-users – without society. We did not just happen to get together to form a society; society was and remains the necessary condition for our very existence as human.

Emile Durkheim (1858–1917) is remembered especially for the force with which he impressed this point upon us.[8] For him the social scientist studies 'social facts', features of human life which cannot be explained in terms of individual psychology because they always exist prior to the individual, who merely passes through them. A social fact can only be explained and accounted for as part of a complete social system, and as having a function in terms of the maintenance of that system. Social facts such as the rules governing language hold generally throughout a society, are transmitted down the generations and are compulsory: there is no opting out of them. They include a stock of basic concepts, or 'collective representations', because society prescribes to us our basic moral principles and categories of thought.

So far as modern politics was concerned, Durkheim was secular, liberal, progressive and republican in outlook. He believed that, as part of nature, society develops in accordance with natural laws.

Population growth produced increasing pressure and competition, which was relieved by an ever-increasing division of labour. In time the growing division of labour makes for a more interdependent and organic kind of society. There is less emphasis on the state's enforcement of the criminal law with harsh penal sanctions, and more emphasis on the state's management of the economy and its role as arbitrator.

For Durkheim, the growing division of labour, and the consequent changeover from harsh retributive moralism to mild economic management, is a movement towards secularism and socialism. In the earliest times almost the whole of the law had been criminal law, and the criminal law was religious law; but in modern society the law has very little expressly religious content left.

It does not follow from this, however, that morality has become unimportant in modern society. Secularization has indeed internalized morality, but morality has not therefore become private, arbitrary or subjective. On the contrary, for Durkheim modern society still has a *conscience collectif*, and the objective authority of morality is still derived from the transcendent moral authority of society itself. Durkheim holds that the purely moral worth of an action cannot be vindicated in terms of its relation, either to my own personal interests, or to the personal interests of any other individual or aggregate of individuals, but only by its relation to the transcendent authority and the *conscience collectif* of society.

It is fair to point out that Durkheim lived before the rise of modern totalitarianism; otherwise he would surely have been careful to safeguard himself against any suggestion that he might be encouraging the cult of Leviathan.

Durkheim treats the body-soul distinction as reflecting the relation of nature to society. Man is a dual being. As a bodily being he is profane, egoistic and subject to sensuous inclination, but society implants in him the sacred power of soul, and makes him capable of conceptual thought and moral action.

Society thus still retains a good deal of its ancient sacred quality even in our modern secular and liberal times. Durkheim's account of how things were at the beginning is given in *The Elementary Forms of the Religious Life: the Totemic System in Australia* (1912: English translation, without the subtitle, 1915). The strength of this celebrated book doubtless lies in its teaching that the key to understanding religion is to see it as the pre-eminent case of a social fact. Hence religion's peculiar authority, generality, persistence, givenness and obligatoriness. It is not an individual intellectual construction, it is not expressive-emotive, and it did not begin either with animism or with theorizing about the grandeur of nature. It is simply a social fact; as much so, and as overwhelmingly so, as language, and indeed rationality itself.

Unfortunately, alongside this great strength there is a corresponding weakness in the book, in that it simply adopts and applies to Australia Robertson Smith's most questionable doctrine, that the original form of religion was a totemic clan cult in which the totem, the clan-god, was the clan itself divinized.

For his account of the Australians, Durkheim relied chiefly on the work of Baldwin Spencer and F. J. Gillen. He describes the aborigines as hunters and foodgatherers, wandering in small hordes around the tribal territory. Each individual, as well as belonging to the horde and a tribe, was also a member of a clan, the clan's badge or totem being some animal, plant or (in a few cases) landscape feature. Each clan member had access to a polished stone or piece of wood bearing an image of the totem. These objects, the churingas, were very holy, had miraculous powers, and were charged up with ancestral souls. The loss of one was a disaster.

The sacred power that indwelt the totem was communicated to all members of the clan. Periodic totemic rites had the function of intensifying group consciousness, charging up the sacredness that bound together all the clansmen in a common divine life. Finally, as the larger social group, the tribe, synthesized the hundreds of clans of which it was composed, so the High God of the tribe synthesized the clan-totems.

Durkheim's interpretation of all this is straightforward. The totem is sacred, protected by taboos and the object of ritual behaviour because the sacred is simply society itself, represented in symbols to its members. The totem is a clan-divinity, the clan itself divinized, and the totemic principle, communicated to each clan-member and symbolized by the icon of the totem that he venerates, is his soul, the totem incarnate in him.

Those who do not like Durkheim's ideas have no difficulty in pointing out innumerable faults in his book, the chief being that 'totemism' as a form of religion, and supposedly the earliest form, has turned out to be a mirage. We cannot prove that the religion of the Australians is primeval, nor that totemism exists to bind people together, rather than being, as has often been argued since Lévi-Strauss, a classification-system. Among hunter-gatherers, anthropologists can quote cases of religion without totemism, of totemism without a clan-system, and of clan-systems without totems. Even among the Australians the clan is not the most important social group, because people spend most of their time dispersed in the hordes.

So the objections run on, and yet one may wonder if in the end they matter very much, for they do not touch Durkheim's real achievement, his characterization of traditional religion, at least, as being a social fact. He was breaking with individualism and the old Cartesian habit of beginning the enquiry from a standpoint within the sphere of individual subjectivity and individual consciousness. Wittgenstein was later to prove with impressive thoroughness that language itself is a 'social fact' in Durkheim's sense. The Cartesian tradition began within the subject, and then tried to construct the public realm as a system of private points of view (Leibniz, Mill). But the new approach argued not only that the attempt to get the public out of the private must fail, but that the private in any case logically presupposes the public. The argument was ultimately Kant's: subjectivity presupposes objectivity, or more fully, objectivity is a transcendental condition of the possibility of there being any subjective experience. This recognition of the logical primacy of the public, entering social science through Durkheim and linguistic philosophy through Wittgenstein, has been crucial for twentieth-century thought.

5

The Archaic Mind

We have seen that Tylor and Frazer regarded the mind of primitive man as having been in many ways like our own. His equipment and his interests were the same, and like us he had sought understanding and control of the world in which he found himself. His misfortune had been that he was immature and hasty. He failed to test his hypotheses with sufficient thoroughness, made mistakes in causal reasoning, and often mistook a mere analogy for an explanation. As a result he fell into errors which have been corrected only by long centuries, and even millennia, of slow progress.

Nevertheless, though immature, his mind and his interests had been of a piece with ours; and we may connect this conviction of continuity with the historicism and evolutionism typical of nineteenth-century culture. People at that time were highly conscious of having come a long way and of standing at the end of a rich and complex process of historical development.

However, from the 1880s a different conviction was taking shape, most conspicuously in the thought of Nietzsche. The new science-based industrial culture was emerging, and it was becoming clear that it represented a violent break with all previous tradition. The chief feature of the new situation was that human thinking and human valuations were much more radically autonomous than ever before, being no longer grounded in any authoritative, coherent and secure vision of the cosmic order. In a science-based culture nothing is sacred because everything is dubitable, truth is fragmentary, disconnected and socially neutral, and understanding is reduced to the mere recognition of regularities. There is a total absence of what ordinary folk variously describe as 'absolutes', 'certainties', Truth with a capital 'T' or Meaning with a capital 'M'. Inevitably, large numbers of mountebank gurus and cults rush in to fill the vacuum, but they are so obviously not the genuine article that they make it only the more clear that our loss is utterly irretrievable, and we must learn to live with a new situation.

After Nietzsche, therefore, there begins a sharp reaction against historicism and against its associated narrative and revivalist art-styles. An art of discontinuity, the Modern Movement, arises. The sense of a qualitative difference between science-based and pre-scientific cultures, and between critical-scientific and all earlier ways of thinking, extends itself into the conviction that the mind of archaic man must have been different in kind from our own. So throughout the present century a line of thinkers has endeavoured to define the difference, and they have had a strong personal and emotional investment in the issue. If only, they thought, we could define what our ancestors were and how they differed from us – or, alternatively, what we are and how we differ from them – then we might be able to understand our own spiritual condition more clearly.[9]

However, we soon run into problems. What is being contrasted with what? Is the contrast between Western and non-Western, modern and traditional, science-based and prescientific, literate and preliterate, industrial and preindustrial, or simply secular and religious? These contrasts do not all quite coincide, as when a Japanese wonders whether for him the great divide is between modern Japan and traditional Japan, or if it is not rather between Japan and the West. Again, many writers set up a sharp confrontation between technologist and tribesman, between the cold, demystified modern universe and the sacred animistic jumble of the tribal universe. European Christians may well wish to protest that this way of setting up the question cuts them out. For through much of human history from antiquity until the day before yesterday, from Thales to Darwin, science, philosophy and theology coexisted in our culture. Christian civilization had at least partially synthesized them – as, in its own area, Islamic culture had also done. The achievement may perhaps be questioned, but it ought not to be eliminated and dismissed by a mere act of definition.

Nor are our issues quite so new as we think. I have watched a F'ang medicine man cast out an evil spirit, and have wondered what to make of a world view and of beliefs so different from my own. But the ancient Israelites in Old Testament times were already trying out a number of hypotheses to explain the status of the gods of other nations. They were perhaps inferior divinities, or demons, or illusions or mere natural forces falsely worshipped: in short, different though the ancient Israelites were from us, both their problem and the hypotheses they advanced to solve it remain perfectly intelligible to us. More generally, the anthropologists' own favoured fieldwork method of participant observation is itself a denial of the discontinuity thesis, for it presupposes that the Western student of a tribal society can in fact learn their language, take part in their way of life, and come to understand their beliefs and world view sufficiently well to be able to expound them in a Western language to a Western audience. In some cases, which are not just jokes but true stories, the anthropologist can do this so successfully that his book is subsequently adopted by the people in question as their bible.

One shift, however, has taken place. I call it the movement to anthropocentrism, and it produces a slight gap between the account the tribesman himself gives of his own religion, and the account given by the Western observer. Briefly, the tribesman's own language will seem relatively more cosmocentric, whereas the observer's explanation will sound rather more anthropocentric.

The reason for this difference of emphasis is to be found in the cultural history of the West. The early and most conspicuous successes of science were in the fields of cosmology and natural philosophy. In those areas science largely took over from religion, with the result that, at least from the time of the rise of pietism and Methodism, Christianity became gradually more anthropocentric in outlook. A good deal of traditional religious language, especially in the Middle Ages, had seemed to have a cosmological meaning – that is, to be describing events out there in the world. But increasingly the tendency was to apply or 'cash' religious language entirely within the sphere of human life and experience. Even idioms which *prima facie* seemed to be cosmological came habitually to be applied within the human sphere. Christianity had of course always been a human life-guidance-system, but now there was a tendency in practice (although this was not acknowledged in theory) for it to be understood simply and solely as an itinerary for human life.

This gradual humanization of religious thought in the West is reflected in the thought of Feuerbach and Durkheim, and it influences the way a Western observer interprets traditional religion. He naturally thinks that although it seems cosmological its real meaning is human, for that is how he has become used to thinking of his own religion.

His argument may go something like this: certainly much of ritual language and action seems, at the 'literal' level of meaning, to be cosmocentric. But the appearance is misleading. In ritual people are not seeking to describe the order in the world in a scientific way; rather, they use ritual to prescribe the future shape of their world. That is, rituals are human activities through which we order our own lives. The difference they make is the difference they make to us. The real meaning of ritual language and action is thus anthropocentric and expressive. Admittedly many believers think that their language makes factual claims about the world, but this is a mistake on their part, arising from a failure to grasp how religiously barren the modern scientific type of factuality is. There can be no religious point in claiming such factuality for our religious assertions.

Thus the way the rise of science has squeezed Western religion, pushing it willy-nilly in an anthropocentric and voluntarist direction, has opened a gap between the way a tribesman sees his own faith and the way an educated Western observer sees it. So far as religion is concerned, we can say that there is at least the following difference between the archaic mind and the modern mind, that whereas archaic man's religion seemed to him to be comprehensive and to fill his whole world, modern man's religion is relatively squeezed and specialized. It may still have, and may rightly have, supreme authority in the shaping of his life, but he cannot now claim that it also provides him with an adequate and factually-correct cosmology.

This, however, is a rather austere and meagre account of the difference between Them and Us. The richest and most romantic account of the difference was given by the French philosopher Lucien Lévy-Bruhl (1857–1939). The best-known of his books are *Les functions mentales dans les sociétés inférieures* (1910: English translation, *How Natives Think*, 1926) and *La Mentalité primitive* (1922: English translation, *Primitive Mentality*, 1923).

Lévy-Bruhl was influenced by Durkheim in holding that the thinking of individuals is determined by the collective representations of the society to which they belong, the collective representations

being themselves in turn shaped by social structures. Thus every sort
of society has its own characteristic mentality.

Societies are classifiable into two main groups, the primitive and
the civilized. In civilized societies people think mainly in terms of
logic and natural causes, but primitives think differently. They are
oriented towards the supernatural in such a way that they tend to see
almost all striking phenomena as manifestations of occult powers.
Their collective representations are, says Lévy-Bruhl, prelogical and
mystical.

By the term 'prelogical' Lévy-Bruhl did not mean illogical.
Primitive thought may be indifferent to our laws of identity and
non-contradiction, and it may envisage a world in which a thing can
both be and not be something other than itself and almost everything
symbolizes something else, a world of innumerable mystical corres-
pondences, affinities, participations and exclusions; but it does not
follow that primitive thought is irrational. It certainly has standards
of coherence and intelligibility, but they are simply different from
ours.

The main reason for the difference is that the collective representations of the primitive make him see his world as being everywhere
permeated by the action of non-sensible forces and powers. Denying
that our Greek ideas of theory and belief are applicable to primitive
thought, Lévy-Bruhl says that beliefs as such arise only rather late in
the development of culture, when perception and representation
have become separated. The primitive does not first have an
experience, and then interpret it in terms of his mystical beliefs.
Rather, his mystical collective representations themselves evoke his
experience and determine the form that it takes. He does not first see
his shadow and then judge it to be his soul; he simply sees his soul.
There is no question for him of a distinction between his experience
and its interpretation, because the interpretation is prior, and
socially given. Concept dominates intuition; perception is moulded
by socially-formed concepts, the collective representations. His
society determines what world he sees.

Lévy-Bruhl's doctrine is assailed from all sides, his opponents
being divided about equally into those who say that it is absurd to
talk as if tribesmen live in a chronic state of mystic inebriation when
in fact for much of the time they are very practically-minded, and
those who say that the primitive mentality is in any case almost as
common among us as it is among tribespeople. Lévy-Bruhl did not in

fact deny either point, for he knew perfectly well that tribesmen can observe their environment very accurately and can make highly-efficient weapons and boats, and he also knew perfectly well that the 'primitive mentality' is far from absent in our own society.

Yet he did not explain himself as clearly as he should have done. Let us, on the basis of what we have said already, explain the mystical participations that surround the 'primitive'. For example, among us many a man participates mystically in his car. He treats it as an extension of himself. Kick it, and he will behave as if you had kicked him. If he drives it into a lamp-post, he will say, '*I* hit a lamp-post', and so on.

Now in traditional society there are many relationships of this kind. For example, a man participates in his own shadow. He will not like you to stick a spear in it, and he will be wary of crossing an open space at mid-day when his shadow will be small and weak. So also a man participates in his child, to such an extent that he may himself take the medicine when the child is sick.

Lévy-Bruhl, insisting that the primitive mentality is in its own terms rational, declared that although a particular custom may seem bizarre in isolation, it is intelligible when seen in its proper context as part of a social system. Let us then examine mystical participations systematically and in context: we list them all, and we find, perhaps, that a man stands in this very special relationship to his name, his shadow, his picture or image, his wives, children and other kinsfolk, his cattle, his land, his totem, his age-set and his chief. It now becomes evident that the whole set of mystical participations that surround a man is simply the sum of his important relationships. Through them he gets his self-esteem, his social personality and identity as the person he is; and a mystical participation is simply a moral metaphor.

This recalls our earlier discussion of the move to anthropocentrism, for we are saying that the tribesman talks as if for him there were some occult bond out there in the world, whereas we prefer to say that his real meaning is human and ethical. But the difference is perhaps not so very great. In modern English culture a familiar example of a mystical participation is the believers' prayer concerning Christ, 'that we may evermore dwell in him, and he in us'. From the point of view of scientific rationality these words seem to describe a rather puzzling geometrical feat, yet during over twenty years in the ministry I have never heard anyone say that he found them difficult to understand. People are aware that in biblical and Christian language the term commonly used for mystical participation is 'indwelling', with mutual or reciprocal indwelling being reserved for the most intimate participation or communion. Its meaning is obviously ethical, and it does not seem to cause any great problems. We simply use it, just as the tribesman does.

If all this is true, then Lévy-Bruhl's doctrine of the primitive mentality needs to be reappraised. It is not after all so odd and objectionable as it at first seems. For all it amounts to is the claim that primitive man's view of the world, his rituals and his typical linguistic idioms are rather more consistently prescriptive, practical and ethical than ours and therefore are more pervaded by rich moral metaphors such as the metaphor of mystical participation, which is common in his world but has become reduced in ours.

However, although the recent rise to dominance of scientific rationality has already significantly reduced our ability to understand the older mentality, the situation is not yet quite desperate. For the greatest of all literary monuments to the prescriptive and ethical-metaphorical view of the world and use of language, the Hebrew Bible, was familiar to everyone until very recently.

Lévy-Bruhl should perhaps be seen as one of the many twentieth-century thinkers who have set up a myth of modern man's divided mind. We distinguish two halves of the mind or two ways of thinking, and then argue that with the way modern culture is developing there is a great danger of our becoming spiritually deformed as one half becomes hypertrophied and the other half remains relatively underdeveloped. Jung, Martin Buber, D. H. Lawrence and many others have preached such a message. In the following list, the first item in each pair represents that which is in danger of becoming over-developed, and the second that which, so we are told, must be brought forward into greater prominence in order to compensate, and to balance the personality: logos and mythos, instrumental and expressive, technical and ritual, masculine and feminine, the Ego and the Unconscious, reason and emotion, I-it and I-thou relationships, logic and mysticism, the rational and the magico-religious, convergent and divergent reasoning, discursive and intuitive thinking, calculation and imagination – and so on, almost indefinitely.

The setting-up of a binary opposition of this kind, by way of defining a matter for thought or initiating a story or message, is so pervasive a feature of human thinking that it is not surprising that

someone should have attempted to build a theory around it. Claude
Lévi-Strauss (1908–) is a theoretical comparative ethnographer in
the tradition of Frazer and Lévy-Bruhl, interested in establishing
universal truths about the human mind.[10] In anthropology he is most
famous for his studies of myth as a clue to the inner workings of the
mind, of totemism because it at once segments society and provides a
simple classification of significant features of the environment, of
kinship because the giving and receiving of women in marriage is the
most primal and powerful form of social communication, and even
of cookery because of what it says about the relation of culture to
nature. In short, Lévi-Strauss sees the myths and institutions of tribal
man as clues to the logic of primitive thought.

His method is in the tradition of the great post-Hegelian thinkers,
especially Marx and Freud. By the use of a specially developed
analytical technique the phenomena are explained as arising from an
underlying and hidden formal structure.

Freud had himself implied that there is an analogy between the self
and society, between the logic of dreaming in the individual and the
logic of myth in society, and between the primary processes in the Id
and the very earliest stages of human thought. It is easy to see how an
ethnographer who admired Freud could believe that by a structural
analysis of myth-logic he could uncover the earliest stages of the
emergence of human thinking out of nature. The most crucial point
that Lévi-Strauss adds to Freud is a much more vivid awareness of
language. It is language by which man the animal has been
transformed into man the social being. So structuralism (like all the
most recent movements in French thought) is highly linguistically
conscious.

From a linguist friend named Jakobson, who has constructed
binary computer-style models of the way the brain functions, Lévi-
Strauss picked up and then developed the idea that the human mind
works by identifying sharp contrasts within experience, and then
seeking to reconcile them. *Distinguir pour unir*. Typical fundamental distinctions are ones God makes to order the world in
Genesis: day and night, Heaven and Earth, land and sea, Sun and
Moon, plant and animal, male and female. Myths are concerned
with these great antitheses, and with a few more, such as culture and
nature, the tame and the wild, the sky and the underworld, left hand
and right hand, life and death, and good and evil. According to Lévi-
Strauss, not only myths, but all other cultural products are elabor-

ations and transformations of polarities or binary contrasts which we have picked out from the field of our experience.

Different cultural products are formed for different purposes. In the face of such life-problems as death, evil and the inequality of the sexes, myths work by publicly displaying the conflicts and by so weaving a tale around them as in varying proportions to explain, justify, validate, reconcile or console.

The method suggests that religions grow as elaborate reconciling metaphors of culture and nature, and of social relations. Its implications are broadly naturalistic and sociological in the style of Durkheim. The programme aims to cut down the pretensions of individual consciousness, and to show instead that all our thinking and cultural life are constrained by deep structural social facts. However, the theory is not precise, rigorous or testable enough to be used by scientific psychologists; and it contains an obvious paradox. It sees society as a system of communication at the social-fact level. But it borrows its account of the code from the computer world, an ultra-Cartesian world, mechanistic, highly conscious, and promising the operator complete rational control over the language he manipulates. It may well be that in our social life we are sending and receiving messages all the time, at a level of which we are unconscious; but if we are indeed doing so, it is surely unlikely that the medium of communication we are using formally resembles a computer language.[11]

PART IV

THE ANTINOMIES OF
RELIGIOUS THOUGHT

I

Historical Succession of Religious Types

Religion has developed historically. We do not say that it has 'progressed'; merely that it has changed. The phenomena are indeed complex, and no two writers can agree on how to define the development. With what schema and with what principles of change shall we work? Nobody is sure. Yet one point is generally conceded: religious change has been brought about by such events as the invention of writing and the emergence of large-scale societies with an ever-greater division of labour. This is a most important recognition, for it grants that religion is a social fact connected with other social facts, in such a way that as they change it must change with them.

We will briefly sketch, not actual phenomena, but a series of ideal types of religion. We do not suggest that there has been any tidy one-for-one replacement during the succession, for in fact the older types have persisted. We acknowledge various debts – to Mircea Eliade, for example, and especially to Robert N. Bellah for his 1964 paper, 'Religious Evolution' – but the story that Bellah tells is here much modified for our own purposes.[1]

Religion, then, consists in a set of symbolic forms and actions by which human beings relate themselves to the fundamental conditions of their existence. Animals just endure the basic limits of life, but man cannot be content with that. He thinks them and represents them symbolically, in such a way that it becomes possible for him to have dealings with them. In this way he is able to transcend them, or at least to gain some measure of freedom in relation to them. Religion is therefore our human way of facing up to, and coping with, the ultimate conditions of our existence.

Are not these ultimate conditions perennial and unalterable? Not quite, for nature, evil, finitude and death themselves do not have fixed natures. They are very diversely perceived at different times, and religious thought and action have taken correspondingly different forms.

In the small-scale societies of preliterate times there was a single cosmos, for the natural world and the world of myth had not yet been clearly separated from each other. Rather, they were aspects of a single totality. That being so, religious thought did not have a perfect World Beyond to look to, and there were no very clear ideas of asceticism or of gaining salvation by escaping from this world to a better one. The dead were not yet sharply divided between the faithful, destined for a blessed immortality, and the faithless, destined for a wretched one. The land of the dead was thought of as being located in some other region of the one cosmos. It might be a happier place than this, but at any rate the dead did not live in a quite different world, of *infinitely* greater value than this world. The general aim of religious action was therefore not to gain promotion to a better world, but rather to maintain cosmic harmony between men and spirits, society and nature, the living and the dead. It was important also to secure needed goods such as good health and children, rain and the harvest.

1. The vital fact about the world-view and the religion of the early hunter-gatherers was that their technology was very simple. Unlike all later human beings, they were not able to surround themselves with a comfortable man-made 'second Nature' in order to defend themselves against wild Nature. As a result they had very little imagery of power and control. Their conceptions both of the cosmos and of the human self were relatively loose-knit and unorganized. So they lacked a proper pantheon of gods linked with the cosmic zones and organized into a graded society, and their spirit-world was instead writhing, chaotic and multifarious – like the cosmos, and like their own souls. Unable to adapt Nature to their own requirements, they were compelled to adapt themselves to Nature. Religious action was therefore not a matter of rational negotiation by prayer and

THE ANTINOMIES OF RELIGIOUS THOUGHT

sacrifice, but rather a matter of ritual identification. You yielded
yourself up to the spirit-being who possessed you. The typical religious professional was therefore the shaman, not the priest, and the
typical religious states were not prayer and contemplation but trance
and ecstasy.

2. With the domestication of animals and plants human control
over nature began to improve. Human life becomes less nomadic, and
more settled and tied in to the annual cycle of nature. The self and the
cosmos become more unified. Now we find that the spirit-beings too
have changed. They are now gods, for their personalities have become
more stable than in the old days, they have more power, they are
assigned to definite cosmic zones and have definite jobs to do, and they
are organized into an intelligible society. All this is a great improvement. It is now possible to do business with the gods, and a regular
communication system, the cult, is established.[2] The typical religious
professional is now the priest, and his chief means of communication
are prayer and sacrifice. The older sort of religious professional lingers
on in the form of the prophet. He is much respected, because people
are nostalgic for the wild ecstasy and immediacy of the older type of
religion, but the new is certainly more orderly and peaceful.

There is just one doubt: because the gods now have so much more
stable, powerful and autonomous personalities it is not possible to be
quite sure of what they are thinking or what their response will be. For
that matter, in this new kind of religion neither is it possible to be quite
sure of the sincerity of the worshipper. There can be no doubt that a
person in a state of ecstasy is sincere, for he has no choice. But the god
cannot be quite so sure about a honey-tongued and careful priest.
With these reciprocal uncertainties new elements enter into religion:
freedom, anxiety, dread, doubt and speculative thought.

3. The religion of the earliest cities was highly theocratic and
cosmological. A new type of person, the peasant, appeared. He no
longer had a complete society of his own around him, but was subject
to an immensely strong external focus of power and sacred authority,
located in the city. The city had been built by the god to be his own
habitation. The temple sanctuary was the place of creation and the
axis of the universe, the cosmology being elaborated in concentric
circles around it. It was the focus: all produce, tribute and pilgrims
gravitated to the centre, and the system of weights and measures, the
calendar, law, money and everything else by which society is ordered
emanated from it.

Human beings are 'the cattle of God', and originally in the Golden Age the gods had indeed lived upon earth and reigned over men in person. However, they had slowly withdrawn. At first they had delegated the day-to-day running of affairs to a college of priests acting on their behalf, the form of government which is properly called hierarchy. But in time the priests were replaced by kings, who were descended from the gods and acted as mediators between gods and men. The king himself might even be seen as a god. The cult was very centralized, for the king was himself the only true priest, the old college of priests being now merely permitted by him to perform some of his religious functions on his behalf.

The ritual was by no means congregational worship, for there was still no laity. The function of religious action was to keep present-day society up to Golden-Age standards, treating the image of the god just as if it were the god himself, still present and reigning in person – which meant treating him just as if he were a king. Daily he was awakened, washed and anointed, dressed and fed. Only at festival times would the common people get a glimpse of him, when he was taken out to receive their acclamations.

4. Grand though it was, city religion eventually provoked a great rebellion out of which the scriptural world faiths developed. A whole series of new ideas and developments appeared in rapid succession. Writing became very much more flexible and widely-available, so that it could now preserve something of the message and even the personality of a great teacher. The individual became much more self-conscious and more concerned about his own personal religious destiny. The first multi-cultural religions appeared, and with them a certain universalism: we meet the conception of man as such, the universal human, for the first time. We also meet the first explicitly religious societies, congregations or brotherhoods, the Jewish syna-gogue and the Buddhist sangha.

However, the most startling innovation was the affirmation of the infinitely superior value of a higher world beyond this present world. Life's chief task and hope was the gaining of a place in that higher world. Other people and institutions could give some vital help and assistance, but in the event whether or not he gained salvation depended upon the individual alone. Anyone, by performing the right exterior and interior religious acts, could secure his own salvation, but nobody could secure anyone else's.

Karl Jaspers saw all the major world faiths as either having appeared, or at least as having been seeded, in an Axial Period that he dated from 800 to 200 BC. The religious thought of this remarkable period was highly individualistic and therefore by implication also democratic in that, so far as life's only ultimately important task was concerned, every single person was on a precisely equal footing. Every other interest in life was radically devalorized in comparison with the supreme task of gaining salvation.

It might be thought that this extreme individualism, egalitarianism and concentration upon the quest for salvation would lead people to conclude that there was no longer any religious justification for inequalities of rank, glory, class and religious status in society. The serious believer should repudiate them – and, for a while it was so. For each of the three greatest universal faiths, Christianity, Buddhism and Islam, began as a simple brotherhood, of poor saints, of monks and of warrior-believers respectively. There was a kind of primitive communism in each faith.

However, this state of affairs did not last, for it soon appeared that an equally persuasive argument could be advanced for the opposite conclusion. If worldly rank and glory were now worthless, why trouble oneself about their existence? Life's only important question is 'What must I do to be saved?', and the answer to it describes a certain transformation of our hearts and our way of life that we must individually undergo. It seems then that we must withdraw from the world, cultivate personal devotion and obedience, and renounce any envious or censorious concern about such irrelevancies as worldly activity, wealth and power. Religion has no special interest either in social inequalities or in social levelling. Its eyes are fixed on another horizon.

The new cosmology and the new concern for personal salvation created (except in Islam, which is a special case) a strong laity distinct from the political society, and clear distinctions between church and state and between the religious and the secular value-scales. But once again, the argument could go two ways. The church could become quietist, admitting its political unconcern and incompetence and confining itself to worship and the pursuit of salvation. But it might also be argued that under the new conditions religion has an even stronger transcendent anchorage than before, whereas politics has been downgraded, has lost its old sacredness and has become a mere matter of temporal expediency. Religion no longer has to validate political authority; quite the opposite, for politics is now exposed to sharp religious criticism from an eternal standpoint that has soared entirely beyond its reach. It is now possible, therefore, for religion to motivate reforms and revolts, and in general to play a much more independent and active role in social life than in the past.

We see here anticipations in the ethical sphere of the antinomies of religious thought that will soon be preoccupying us. Here is another one: in the books of Judges and Samuel there is evidence that some people argued with Gideon that because God was Israel's true king the nation ought not to have any human king, whereas others argued that God's kingship over Israel ought to be visibly bodied forth in a city, a Temple, and a king who by a special covenant with God would reign as God's favoured son and servant.

Nowadays, when we are readier to admit our inability to build any unified system of doctrine – and perhaps even to admit that such a thing would be undesirable, anyway – it is easier for us to recognize that the whole of Christian ethics is affected by such antinomies. Many of them, such as the antinomy of the active and the contemplative lives, and the antinomy of the affirmation and the rejection of images, are paralleled in other religious traditions. Before we pass on, we note also that the various ethical and spiritual antinomies so far mentioned are interconnected. Note too that just one genuine antinomy (in the strong Kantian sense) is enough to prove that systematic theology is impossible.

5. After the burst of creativity that gave rise to the major world faiths there was a period of reaction and stagnation. Something like civic religion was reinstated when faiths as diverse as Islam, Christianity and Buddhism were successfully, and largely unprotestingly, conscripted into endorsing societies of the feudal type.

6. The next major change began towards the end of the Middle Ages, not only in Christianity but to some extent in Eastern faiths as well. In spirituality, salvation was internalized and made immediate again. In ethics there was a turning to this world. Both the mystic and the popular teacher rebelled against the elaborate bureaucracy of salvation, the objectified and graduated apparatus of the sacred. As salvation became directly and personally seizable, individualism was restored and the world desacralized. From now on the hierarchy, the hereditary aristocracy and kingship steadily decline, and religion becomes more lay, more voluntary and active.

A highly sacralized society does not leave much scope for innovative religious activity, because there is so much holiness

around that it makes the world immovable. The drastic secularization of the world in early modern times greatly increased the scope
for religious action. In Christianity it became for the first time
possible to see a fully active life in the world – a politically,
economically and sexually active life – as an integrally holy life.

7. The course of the argument suggests that we may end this sketch
by characterizing the religious situation today as follows: older
religious world-views still survive but are now believed only in a
bracketed or ironical way. The dualism, going back to the Indian
ascetics and Plato, between this fleeting world here below and the
eternal and perfect world above has by now wholly broken down. It
is replaced by a simple moral contrast between the way the world is
and the way it ought to be. Religion has thus become internalized,
moralized, voluntary and ethical. People see their life-task as that of
becoming better and more mature individuals, and doing a little to
make the world a better place and not a worse one for those who
come after.

Accordingly, there is at present a good deal of interest in
consciousness-raising, in the quest for meaning and in mysticism,
and also strong support for innumerable good causes to do with
peace, human rights, the environment and so forth. But the old-style
sacred is gone, swallowed up into the profane. Even where it still
exists, it does not help religion any longer because it always inhibits
human action and criticism, whereas what today heightens religion
and gives it most scope is the unhindered confrontation between
passionate religious idealism and a fully-plastic because fully-
secularized world. The more secular the world is, and the more
straightforwardly we see religious belief as commitment to a set of
ideals and not a set of facts, the purer and stronger will religion be.

So much for a preliminary characterization: let it stand, for the
present. The discussion in this chapter has sought to establish a
different point: the history of religions has shown that religion has a
history. Even today, most people hesitate to acknowledge the
implications of that very simple proposition.

Perhaps they are right to be reluctant, for what are those
implications? If religion has a history, then it is human. It is not a
body of immutable and supernaturally-certified truths that fell from
the sky. It is a creative and expressive human activity, which quite
properly takes different forms in different epochs.

2

Possible Forms of Religion

We have reviewed seven types of religion that have appeared in the course of history. Now we cut the cake in a different way, attempting by a simple formal analysis to display the chief possible kinds of faith or philosophy of life. To do this we set up two axes.

The vertical axis runs between the two poles of world-affirmation and world-transcendence. By 'world-affirmation' I mean that movement in religious thought which says 'Yes' to this world because it must, knowing no other; and for which our life is so obviously embedded in Nature and dependent on natural cycles that it is evident that the social order must be conformed to the cosmic order.

This way of thinking is both old and new. Older forms of it might be called paganism, nature-religion or natural law; newer forms might be called naturalism, environmentalism or ecological humanism. At any rate, to those who think like this it is obvious that no religious or ethical project whatever can be either truthful or realistic unless it grows out of and is continuous with life's own perennial self-affirmation.

Yet there is an opposed mood of 'world-transcendence', in which the spirit chafes against the physical and moral limits of natural life. A certain kind of psychological inflation or soaring leads us to believe ourselves capable of perfection, infinity, eternity. Our highest spiritual fulfilment cannot be attained while we remain tied to temporal succession and biological life. The spirit yearns for cosmic deliverance, release from nature, and final victory over evils without and within.

So much for the vertical axis: the horizontal runs between the poles of history and eternity. With history we link the ideas of linear time, progress, providence and the habit of locating the objects of hope in the temporal future. So 'History' means a kind of religion or view of life that has an historical hope, and looks to the future and to God the Lord of history for the fulfilment of its advent longings. Salvation is to be achieved not by escaping from time, but precisely through the movement of the historical process towards its own ordained and glorious consummation. This view of life therefore assigns a high value to this-worldly and social action, to striving for betterment and to looking forward in hope; for however much it may be said that the future consummation is inevitable or is in God's hands, there is always a good deal that human beings can do to help things along.

Yet there is an opposite mood. We use 'Eternity' in a rather general sense to indicate the direction of religious attention towards what is stable, unchangeable and non-temporal. It may also include cyclical time as the opposite of linear time, the circle being an image of eternity. For many, this kind of security and incorruptibility is religion's essential concern, and it belongs not only to the eternal world and the sacred but to tradition and to the faith itself. Faith hopes for *rest*, the rest of God, the saints' everlasting rest, because many forms of Christianity, as well as of other religions, disparage what is transient and urge us to look to eternal things. Historical change as such, they declare, can never bring anyone even so much as one inch nearer to God. Suppose that the most far-fetched fantasies of communists and anarchists were realized and the perfect society came on earth at last: would not all the ultimate questions of life still remain quite untouched and press upon people more urgently than ever? As soon as they had everything and there was no more need for striving, would not people at once be paralysed with boredom, dissatisfaction and vague infinite longings? Only the eternal can finally satisfy the soul.

Now we construct a diagram, and label the resulting quadrants as follows:

World-transcendence

|
3. Eschatological hope | 2. Indian 'release'
|
History_____|_____Eternity
|
4. Marxist humanism | 1. Archaic timeless
| harmony with Nature
|

World-affirmation

There is one further detail to add: with each basic philosophy of life there is associated a distinctive form of selfhood, still to be described.

1. The phrase, 'Archaic timeless harmony with Nature' evokes in the first place a form of life very common in pre-literate and therefore pre-historical times. There is no very strong sense of linear time, and society is merged into Nature. The self is rather dormant, undifferentiated and loose-knit: we will describe its state as 'dreaming innocence', to borrow a phrase from Paul Tillich.

A number of moderns are interested in the thought of returning to this spirituality, and a glance at the diagram to see what they oppose will indicate the main lines of their argument. They reject 'History', arguing that the Earth's resources are finite, and that a sustainable society must therefore be based on renewable resources – which means natural cycles, and the deliberate abandonment of our Western ideas of linear time and indefinite future progress. Secondly, they also reject transcendence, partly in the conviction that all metaphysical ideas of transcendence have now broken down, and partly because in any case they suspect that the entire transcendence-theme was never genuinely religious. It was just an ideology of conquest.

The forces that today press us towards a new kind of biological religion are much stronger than most people yet realize. Darwin's religious impact in making us feel an intense sense of kinship with all life, and in awakening in us a truly passionate love for the natural environment, is still increasing steadily.

2. 'Indian release' is a more familiar spirituality, introduced to the West by Schopenhauer and now very widely diffused. Schopenhauer himself thought that Idealist philosophy had prepared the way for it

by showing us to what an extent the sensuous, phenomenal world around us is mere 'representation', the creation of our own minds. The Kantian doctrine of the ideality of time disposed of the naïve idea that there is something religiously to be hoped for through the mere tick-tock passage of linear time. Nineteenth-century humanitarianism was strong enough, even in a misanthropic old villain such as Schopenhauer, to show that all human life is incurably pervaded by suffering. Finally, the new psychological consciousness of the age revealed what a fragmentary, irregular chain of experiences the illusion we call 'the self' really is.

For all these reasons the turn to the East seemed inevitable. The form of selfhood associated with it can soon be worked out. Surrounded by evil and illusion, we seek detachment from the world, and even inner detachment from the illusions of selfhood. So the highest development of this spirituality is the *anatta*, the 'no-self' doctrine of the Buddha.

3. Eschatological hope is the distinctive and very remarkable spirituality of Judaism and Christianity, the advent yearning for a great supernatural Deliverance that is to arrive in due time, at the End of time. Expectant confidence in the imminent coming of a transcendent and final salvation creates an intense and ardent anticipatory joy.

The real thing has been rare even in Christian history, and later faiths that have emerged within the same tradition of prophetic monotheism, such as Islam, Sikhism and the Bahai, show less and less of it. Yet even where the pure kingdom-expectation is no longer to be found, something of its flavour may still survive by having spilled over into neighbouring areas of religious life. The Advent joy may be seen on Easter and Christmas nights, in individuals facing death, and in time of persecution.

So distinctive is the Christian hope – historical, supernatural and, above all, *anticipated* – that there have been attempts to transpose it out of its original theological context so as to make it more widely available. The two most notable are by the Spaniard Miguel de Unamuno (*Del Sentimiento Trágico de la Vida*, 1912; *The Tragic Sense of Life*, 1921) and the German Ernst Bloch (*Das Prinzip Hoffnung*, 1959, [2]1967). But inevitably neither writer was able to find a modern counterpart for the primitive Christian's factual confidence. Each of them was left looking like a greyhound straining after a rabbit he can never catch, which is not at all the same thing.

The Christian and Jewish form of selfhood we describe as ethical individuation, because in Jeremiah, Jesus and Paul, and elsewhere the perfected society of the New Covenant is envisaged as a society in which every single individual is to be ethically perfected and to have his own unique god-relationship.

4. The last kind of spirituality we have dubbed marxist humanism, although it includes every modern philosophy of life which is secular, activist, optimistic and progressive. To understand it we need to reckon with the radically man-centred world view that developed during the eighteenth century and began to prevail everywhere after the French Revolution. In the novel, in naturalistic drama and in related art-forms we see the arrival of a time in which the world of human activity and communication has become autonomous and virtually self-existent. Everything else has become a mere offshoot from it. The world is purely human, and there is nothing left for us to reckon with except the human: the human world is subject to no standards but ones that it has evolved and imposed on itself.

This kind of humanism is philosophically very realist, believing in matter and in linear time. It is also highly historicist, treating all ideas to do with the individual, his subjectivity, his salvation and his moral and religious values as mere transient social products. The marxist is not notably interested in the rights or the destiny of the individual. His point of view is very public and objective, so that the form of selfhood we may associate with him is post-religious and post-individualist. It is simply wholehearted commitment to the political struggle for social betterment. I suggest calling it 'publicity', because for it only public and objective action counts; subjectivity is of no interest.

To recapitulate, then, the four forms of selfhood are labelled dreaming innocence, no-self, ethical individuation and publicity, respectively. They are naturalistic, mystical, moralistic and political, in that order.

The question now arises, are there grounds for choosing between these different spiritual stances? Or is the position that we can find good arguments for each of them, but no certain way of knocking out any of them?

There is little value in pointing out that the typologies in this chapter and the last are crude and over-simplified. To say that is merely to defer answering the question.

3

The Antinomies

In the past I have given two answers to the question just formulated, neither of which now satisfies me. The first answer is liberal and historicist. We tell the long story of the ways in which religion has in the past taken different forms under different cultural conditions, and we tell it in such a way that by the end it becomes clear what new shape is currently crystallizing out. There was an example in the first chapter of this section. We were roughly following Robert N. Bellah's scheme – American, liberal and protestant – and we ended up with something like Californian pluralism and the triumph of the voluntary principle. We would, wouldn't we? But there are other ways of telling the story. The Japanese philosopher Keiji Nishitani believes that, having reached nihilism in the past century, Western thought has now nowhere to go but towards Buddhism; and there are many people in the West who would agree with him.[3] By contrast, Lloyd Geering, in *Faith's New Age*, ends with Nietzschean heroic humanism;[4] and others again will see a strong case for ending with marxism.

In short, historicism will not help. Unless along Hegelian lines we can prove that the history of thought must follow just one path (and there is no chance of that), then everyone will inevitably tell the story in such a way that his own favoured option shines out as the obvious next step – and we will not have any way of deciding between the rival versions of the story so as to see where to go next.

The second unsatisfactory solution comes from Kierkegaard. In his marvellously original *Either/Or* of 1843, Kierkegaard has already grasped the fundamental religious problem of the modern period: we cannot transcend the limits of human thought and experience, and we will therefore never be able to appraise our situation from outside with absolute objectivity. We do not have either the transcendent vantage-point or the logically independent criteria for assessment that would be needed. Instead we find that we are always immersed in some particular moral world, and we know that there is more than one of these moral worlds. Each moral world has its own standards and appears to its own denizens to be reasonably coherent and complete. Furthermore, since every value already belongs within one world or another, we cannot make any moral comparison between the worlds except from a standpoint that is already committed to one of them.

It begins to look, then, as if it is logically impossible that we should ever have adequate reasons to justify our original and primal choice of our values and of the moral world we choose to inhabit. Once we are in a moral world and have values, then we have a standpoint and criteria and can talk about giving reasons. But we cannot have reasons for our basic values, for it is the job of our values to give us reasons, and not the other way round.

In spite of what people say, Kierkegaard was a Hegelian, and his answer owes much to Hegel. Hegel had been the first philosopher to recognize that there are many different possible forms of consciousness, each of which is able to build a more or less complete and self-contained world around itself. His method was to arrange all the possible forms of consciousness in a series. He then sets out to explore each of them from within, and by various devices seeks to show why and how the transition must be made to the next.

It is noticeable that Hegel's scheme has values built in from the outset. The various forms of consciousness are designed as stations on the march of Spirit towards absolute knowledge. Each has its place in the line, and Hegel's scheme always prescribes what the next step has got to be. The step-by-step ascent is a climb up a value-scale.

Borrowing no more than he needs from this, Kierkegaard has only a very simple series of stages on life's way: the aesthetic, the ethical, the religious and the Christian. They are the poet, the judge, the platonist and the man of faith, and in terms of traditional preaching and apologetics they are the natural man, the Pharisee, the religious pagan and the true Christian. In short, these are not fully independent moral worlds because we, like Kierkegaard, already had them ranked in an ascending series in our heads.

Following Hegel, and in some respects even improving on him, Kierkegaard explores each particular form of consciousness and way of life in very great detail. Eventually, of course, it runs into frustration, absurdity, despair or contradiction, and the spirit is forced somehow to make the jump to the next world in line. The crucial point about the method of argument is that it is, in the jargon, *immanent* or internal. The exposure of the insufficiency of the aesthete's way of life has to be carried out from within that way of life, without appealing to anything that the aesthete does not himself already recognize as part of his own moral world. Kierkegaard has to use strategy: he dons a mask and pretends to be an aesthete or whatever, in order to subvert a world from within. He is a fifth-columnist.

A difficulty needs to be mentioned. If the presence of tragic contradictions within a way of life is a sign that it is breaking down and we will soon be forced to leap out of it into another one, then what are we to make of the appallingly riven, tragic and tormented picture of Christian faith that Kierkegaard gives in the writings of his last two years?

The Kierkegaardian solution to our problem of justification without transcendence runs as follows: in the modern world we realize that no old-style absolute justification of religious belief, from metaphysics or from revelation or both, can any longer be given. We know instead that there are various distinct coherent faiths and philosophies of life, and no intellectually and morally privileged external vantage-point from which to compare them and pass objective judgment upon them. However, it need not follow that our basic beliefs and value-commitments must be irrational, for in fact we can do without any external vantage-point. A rational judgment about a way of life can be made upon the basis of a purely immanent examination of it, investigating it from within and on its own terms. And if we use our imaginations, listen sympathetically and so forth, a rational comparison of several different ways of life can also be made, by exploring each in turn immanently and describing each in its own terms. Indeed, since Kierkegaard's day anthropologists, phenomenologists of religion and others have been learning to do just that.

With Kierkegaard the Copernican revolution – 'there is no privileged vantage-point from which we can judge objectively which of the religions is true' – finally struck religious thought. Contrary to what people say, Kierkegaard was battling, in the face of this new Copernican insight, to save the rationality of religious belief. The question is, was he successful?

Until recently I thought so, but now I have doubts, for as we have suggested Kierkegaard makes things much easier for himself than they can be for us. He trades more than he realizes on the fact that when we read him we already know what the answers are supposed to be. We know that the aesthete is meant to run into despair, and where he will have to turn; and we know that when the Christian is equally tormented – well, that is what it is to share Christ's sufferings. There is no question for the Christian of moving on, because he is already at the top of the tree. The stages on life's way as Kierkegaard describes them have been tacitly pre-arranged in an ascending series, with a great many assumptions and values built in. His cast of characters and their fates are derived from a long and familiar tradition of preaching and moralizing. We already know the answers, because we have read John Bunyan and William Law's *Serious Call*, and the rest.

But the spiritualities described in our last chapter are very much more disparate, and do not come pre-arranged in a series. From the studies of social psychologists we know that what it feels like to the convert to move dramatically from Christianity to marxism is just the same as what it feels like to move equally dramatically in the opposite direction. For Hegel and Kierkegaard the arrows all pointed one way, onwards and upwards, but for us they point all ways. This fact raises questions for us that Kierkegaard did not face. One we have alluded to already: Western Christianity is a psychologically very 'hot' religion that imposes severe stress on the serious believer. We are taught to think of this as a sharing in the sufferings of Christ, and to see it as a privilege. But many cases, including Kierkegaard himself, become very extreme. At what point do we cease to regard the psychic stress as religiously valuable and instead rebel against it; and if so, what do we do – change the faith so as to cool it down, or leave it in favour of a less heated tradition such as Buddhism?

Hegel and Kierkegaard each had an ascending scale, arrows pointing just one way, and tacitly-included values to help them along. We do not. They, like most of the great Central European geniuses, were Lutherans raised on the Greeks and the Bible, and committed to what we called 'ethical individuation' as the form of selfhood they aimed at. Today that can no longer be taken for granted. What we can say with confidence about the human condition is so meagre that it does not allow us to eliminate any of the possibilities mentioned in the last chapter: the antinomies of religious thought arise because we can see a case for every major option, and there is nothing that we are so sure of that we can use it to rule out any major option.

It is not difficult to see why this has happened. The cultural has grown bigger and bigger, and the natural has grown smaller and smaller. Nowadays all ideas of history and eternity, of world-affirmation and world-rejection, are alike just cultural constructions. There is nothing that is 'naturally', objectively or metaphysically the case, in such a way that it clearly falsifies one particular view of life as being factually wrong. If we had them, objective metaphysical truths would enable us to rule out a few of the possibilities. But we have not. Instead, we can see only how the various particular conceptions work out within the forms of life they belong to. From such a starting-point there seems to be no way of avoiding the conclusion that almost any and every faith has its own kind of aesthetic beauty, and its own power to make people such that for them it is true. It works, it is something wonderful and something that people live by – what more can there be to say? But when we have reached that opinion, we have become so broad-minded that it is hard to see how we can still commit *ourselves*. Any religion we follow zealously enough will so influence us that our own lives will seem to us to confirm its truth; so which shall we follow? No rational basis for choice seems to be left to us.

We have already indicated very briefly the case for each of the four spiritualities or religious styles, so I shall prove the antinomies by making out cases for each of the four poles of our axes.

With the triumph of Darwin and scientific naturalism, with the end of mind-body dualism and belief in life after death, *world-affirmation* is surely the only possible, and even the only intelligible spiritual stance left to us. I am now so completely identified with my life and my world that outside their scope there is nothing at all for me, not even nothingness. I cannot do other than say 'Yes' to my life's own battling self-affirmation. The best life is just the fullest, the longest, the most prolific, active and generous.

The counter-argument is that the very scientific naturalism, which decade by decade circumscribes us more tightly, makes a spirituality of *world-transcendence* essential if spiritual, if moral, and if even the most basic human values are to be saved. There is a danger that scientific naturalism will lead people to think of themselves as mere machines, programmed by their biology and by society. A spirituality of world-transcendence need not necessarily involve supernatural beliefs, but it must insist that a properly human life is possible only if we posit and pursue certain spiritual values which transcend what is given within the world view of scientific naturalism. And if the pursuit of those values calls for some degree of asceticism or even denial of our own life-impulses, then that cannot be helped; for the essence of the matter is that you are not fully human unless there is something that is dearer to you than your own life. So the world-transcendence theme maintains that the human does not get constituted at all until we refer to something that goes beyond the world view of scientific naturalism.

Turning now to the History-Eternity axis, we recall that by *history* we meant the way of thinking that sees our life as embedded in a temporal process moving towards a future consummation. The Judaeo-Christian and the Marxist traditions both affirm the primacy of action to realize values. For both, man is an historical, striving being who looks to the future for the fulfilment of his hopes, and who by his action continually changes himself and his world as he co-operates with History, Providence or God.

The case for this view of life begins by pointing out that we are animals, mobile organisms. It is our nature to be constantly active in pursuing our needs, tending what we care for, fulfilling our hopes and desires, and carrying out our plans and projects. These things give worth to life, and without them we have no reason to live. Accordingly we must picture that which gives ultimate worth to our life as a supreme purpose and object of hope and desire, to whose historical attainment we can contribute by our own ethical activity.

The counter argument insists that the great metaphysical limitations that encompass our lives can never be altered by the mere passage of time, nor by human ethical activity. They are just the same for us as they were for our palaeolithic ancestors, and they will be still the same for our remotest descendants. No amount of activity on our part will alter them. Furthermore, all ideas of meaning, purpose and a moral order in the world are simply human and cultural. They are in no way objectively embedded in the nature of things. There is no moral world-order, so there is no way in which the mere passage of time could of itself accomplish anything towards fulfilling any purpose, or making things any better. Purely objectively, the world is just 'white noise', and entirely devoid of structure or meaning.

It may be replied that the previous argument maintained only that linear, historical time is a religiously-advantageous representation; and that for scientific naturalism the world is rather more than mere white noise.

But these two points only make matters worse. Scientific naturalism, if true, invades our own behaviour and our thinking and threatens to rob them of significance; and if the idea of a Good Time Coming is objectively illusory, then where is the value of holding on to it? It would seem therefore that the only way we can make contact with religious values is not by activity but by inactivity, silence and cessation. Religion is after all not about the changing but about the changeless, and the distinctively religious virtues are not the active but the contemplative virtues. Such is the case for the standpoint of *eternity*.

From this discussion of the antinomies of religious thought one dominant theme emerges. From the ethico-religious standpoint there is little difference between nihilism and scientific naturalism. Both are equally bankrupt so far as morality and religion are concerned. The outcome either way is that there is no basis out there in the objective nature of things for claiming that any one spiritual stance or philosophy of life is more appropriate than any other. Each faith is free to make itself plausible by building a world to which it is itself evidently the most appropriate response. Nor is there anything wrong with this circularity: the objective world has become so meagre and therefore so plastic that the various religions and philosophies of life are at liberty to mould it into whatsoever shape they please. They take full advantage of this liberty, and are quite right to do so – provided that they do not simultaneously claim the old correspondence type of truth. Now that a faith has become a creative project for fashioning the world in a certain way, it should be spoken of as good or bad, like art, rather than as true or false. Different faiths are like rival plans that have been submitted for an architectural competition. Some of the designs may look a whole lot better than others, but until the building is built there isn't anything there for any of them to be true or false *of*.

The lack of prior and external controls on religious thought therefore forces us to see religion as a creative and expressive human activity, a proposal to build something rather than a response to or description of something that is already in place. And our problem is that we have far too many proposals and far too few well-established and agreed criteria for deciding on their merits. Besides, the judges are also entrants.

A second difficulty that we have also noticed already is that the various basic options can no longer be arranged in a sequence or ascending order of merit, in the style of Hegel and Kierkegaard. They have become quite disparate and incommensurable.

Finally, there is a third and clinching point. Historically one of the functions of theology has been to crystallize in words the major religious issues and options. We have been reasonably confident that language could pin down the various positions that may be taken. But can it? When in the last chapter we distinguished four principal forms of spirituality and of selfhood, many readers must have wanted to object that all four of them have been found in Christianity alone. The dreaming innocence of a self immersed in nature's rhythms is exemplified in the peasant Christianity of Eastern Europe in the old days; many mystics of the fourteenth to sixteenth centuries ran very close to Buddhism; and a militantly active left-wing Christianity is prominent today, as it has often been in the past.

Nor is my typology the only one that is open to this kind of objection. Far from it: the objection has probably been made to every typology that has ever been produced, for even a modest knowledge of church history equips one to produce from the tradition exotic examples of all extremes. Does the language of Christian theology, then, clearly exclude anything, or not? One may well wonder, for the very rapid disintegration of the old Christian metaphysics that has taken place during the past thirty years has left theological language looking so intolerably hazy and ill-formed that one can make nothing (or anything) of it and do nothing (or anything) with it.

I am not here speaking primarily of the positivist doctrine that theological language has no meaning because it is not empirically verifiable. That is wrong because it suggests that the language seems at first to be perfectly in order, and only later is discovered to be untestable. Our real difficulty is, unfortunately, much more serious than that. Wittgenstein was perhaps the first to feel it: it is that from the outset we cannot get a hold of the language, for it is so vague, confused and ill-disciplined that it merely gives us a headache. It pins nothing down, cuts nothing out, and much of it is not properly tied in to actions.

This collapse of the language of dogmatic theology (not, be it noted, the language of *religion*) is a very recent phenomenon. There is, I believe, no case of our kind of puzzlement before the First World War. Nietzsche was very clever and phenomenally sensitive to language, but he does not complain that he cannot understand the language of theology. On the contrary, though he hates it, its meaning is perfectly clear to him. By contrast, Wittgenstein was highly religious and very much wished to be a believer – even, you might say, in his own purely practical way, *was* a believer – but he was tormented by his own inability to understand many of the leading doctrines. His search for a purely silent and practical religion, without dogma or theory, was an attempt to skirt the insuperable difficulty. And, I suggest, the difficulty that he felt so acutely in the 1930s is now commonplace among us.

Today there are many of us who are religious, but are dissatisfied with all the currently-available forms of religion and seek to articulate something new. But we are in the absurd position that the general breakdown of theological language, especially obvious since about 1960, has left us without any precise vocabulary in which to articulate our concerns. Because of it, there was already in Wittgenstein himself a rather sad strain of religious quietism and impotence, connected with his habit of declaring that the meaning of religion is in the end ineffable.

We cannot be content with such a conclusion. If we complain that religion and theology are nowadays corrupt; if we complain that our culture has become so pluralistic and slovenly that all belief is now ironical and no genuine religion is left any more (and we do make these complaints) – then we cannot merely declare the secret of religion ineffable and lapse into silence. We have to do more than that. Somehow, we have to find words to describe a form of religious existence that resolves the antinomies.

PART V

I HAVE SAID, YE ARE GODS

I

Out of Nothing

For us, the first and hardest truth to accept now is that *the world*, as an objective, ready-ordered cosmos out there and independent of our minds, has come to an end. Since we became fully aware first of society and then of language, we have come to recognize that for us there can only be *our world*, the world that is generated by our language, our knowledge-systems and our practices. *Our world* is, when we pause to think, obviously the only world that could be available to us, and the only world we can reckon with and act upon. And *our world* is something that we ourselves have constituted. It owes its massiveness and its appearance of objectivity to the fact that we have evolved it collectively over the millennia. It is as vast and extraordinary a construction as language itself: it is indeed a great shadow cast by language. It is what-language-is-about, mythically projected out and reified. It is a stupendous work of folk art. It seems objective to us, but its objectivity is sociological: it is such a huge, unconscious and collective product that even the most creative of us makes only the tiniest dent in it. So far as the individual is concerned, it makes him far more than he makes it.

Nevertheless, as it rolls on the millions of us gradually change it. Specialized bits of it such as the natural sciences may change very rapidly indeed, and even the world embedded in our ordinary language, the everyday world, changes perceptibly over a lifetime. But what brings home to us most effectively the fact that our world really is *our* world is the great diversity of ways in which different societies construct their worlds. Naturally each society seeks to impress upon its own members a sense of the sacred authority and inevitability of its own vision of the world, so that within each society there is a strong tendency to equate *our* world with *the* world. But we now find this less easy to accept, for we see that there are too many such worlds, and they change too fast.

Yet if the only world there can be for us is *our world*, and there are many such worlds, then what is our world made of? Here we show a due humility. We are only human, and our world that we have together constituted cannot be made of beings. It is in fact made only of rules, rules that guide all practice, including linguistic practice, and therefore generate meanings.

At first sight, the thesis that human beings have built their world around themselves out of nothing but rules seem amazing. Nietzsche, in line with the heroic individualism of his general outlook, argues that we make by making metaphors, and puts the creative artist at the centre of his account. He was not so concerned with the process by which a metaphor becomes public property, 'the rule', thinking of it merely as a debasement. And at this point he for once missed something. For a game is an obvious, powerful and persuasive example of how a group can create an absorbing, value-rich and purposive world out of nothing, merely by evolving among themselves a set of rules and then following them with religious punctiliousness. No English speaker should need to be told what intense, life-enriching dedication and seriousness of purpose can go into a game. It is said that there have been earnest Continental philosophers who have complained that man is a futile project and that human existence is devoid of meaning. Such philosophers should study the way in which the Englishman innocently creates values, meaning and an aim in life for himself out of nothing, merely by drawing up the rules of games and codes of sportsmanship. Indeed, one of them once did so, and drew the conclusion that all life was like that.

I dare to say that critical thinking requires us to give up ontology; to stop thinking in terms of Being and instead to learn to think always in terms of rules and meanings. So, for example, we give up any inclination to ask if God exists or not, and instead rigorously confine ourselves to asking what rules govern the use of the word 'God'. What job does the word do now? Is it just an expletive, is it used merely to add emphasis, or does it do something distinctive in shaping our practice?

More advanced students – in fact, only *very* advanced students – may as an exercise try to treat themselves in the same way. What human nature is, is also something that is conventionally established; and what I am as an individual user of language is given just by my relative position in the great communication-network that is the human realm. That is all: the individual will in due course have to be demythologized as well.[1]

Many people regard the changeover from the old mythic cosmos made of solid Being, the cosmos of religious and of metaphysical realism, to the new cosmos which is going to be nothing but a very large and fluid body of manmade rules – they regard this changeover as a process of loss. They feel bad about it.

I take as an example the words of the painter Francis Bacon, from a 1962 interview. Bacon has been talking about his own relationship with Velasquez, and in particular about why a certain very intense combination of realism and profundity was still just possible for figures such as Velasquez and Rembrandt, but is not possible today Bacon is of course a romantically pessimistic atheist, who is entirely conscious that his own trick is to make art out of despair:

> I think that man now realizes that he is an accident, that he is a completely futile being, that he has to play out the game without reason. I think that even when Velasquez was painting, even when Rembrandt was painting, they were still, whatever their attitude to life, slightly conditioned by certain types of religious possibilities, which man now, you could say, has had completely cancelled out for him. . . . You see, all art has now become completely a game by which man distracts himself. . . . What is fascinating now is that it's going to become much more difficult for the artist, because he must really deepen the game to be any good at all.[2]

To spectators of his work, Bacon is in fact himself clearly in some sense a religious artist, but here he himself links religion with the realism we have lost. He says in effect that even as late as the seventeenth century religion could still nourish an artist, giving him an ontological assurance and weight that have since been lost. Without the old sources of nourishment, great art becomes more difficult. The artist has to 'deepen the game'. But the game is only a game, played out against a background of utter meaninglessness.

Bacon has described how he himself works in a state of despair. He may use drink or drugs to make himself despair of himself, so that he can get free of himself. When he thinks he will never do it and might as well do *anything* – then, by a grace, the painting starts to come, out of despair and nihility.[3]

Bacon is right to suggest that the old sense of reality that people used to have was of religious origin. It was an overspill from the Sacred. In archaic times, the Sacred was overwhelmingly and annihilatingly real and objective. The book of Exodus can still make the reader shiver at the super-intense concentration of holy Being with which it is charged. And in a religion-based culture this sacred Being spilled over into holy spaces and seasons, objects and persons, gradually diffusing objective reality through the social world. Hence the idea that God creates the world, his infinite Being having the power to call finite beings into existence. It certainly has: so great is the power of religion to generate ontological conviction that the philosophers were able to trade for centuries on ideas of being, objectivity and reality that were in fact nothing but faint shadows of the mighty religious phenomenon that stood behind them. The truth only emerged when the Sacred, the Holy, finally vanished – and *the world* vanished with it, leaving only games.

Bacon is of the same generation as Beckett and Sartre, born in the first decade of the century and growing up with it, and telling the story of where we are now in such a way as to emphasize the magnitude of our loss. But he could have told the story in a very different way. For consider the human situation as twentieth-century unbelief pictures it: we are confronted by nothingness. The earth is without form, and void. Experience is a featureless waste, but we are to make sense of it. We do this by establishing certain grand oppositions, contrasts or distinctions. We set them over against each other, interacting with each other. We lay down the law, we evolve the rules by which our world is to be ordered and given meaning. Within this increasingly complex, dialectical and rule-governed structure, we begin to prescribe purposes and ordain a story of our own prospective deeds and aims. Values and goals emerge.

No doubt it is strange that we are in this position, and even stranger that we are able collectively somehow to do all these marvellous things. But why should we see this position that we are in as being peculiarly novel and desperate? For it is after all precisely the position in which we always imagined our creator-gods to have been at the beginning; and we never supposed that it might have been terrible for *them* to be confronted by pure chaos, and to have the task of so imposing distinction and rule upon it as to convert it into a familiar, habitable and meaningful cosmos. They just do it, for that is the way they are.

Let us see if we can imagine a god with doubts. He says to himself, 'The world is meaningless and my life is meaningless. Here am I, confronted by chaos and by the task of spinning order, purposes and values out of my own entrails like a spider. How am I to do it, and what do I live for? Perhaps my *ennui* and sense of meaninglessness would be overcome if I had a God-Squared, a gods' God to live for and give me worth. Please, is there a God for gods?'

Now that is surely an absurd imagining and one which can only open an infinite regress. If meaning and value always need to be antecedently provided by a higher-level being, then God will surely need a God-Squared to give his life meaning, as he gives meaning to ours. But the truth is that God never was a mere second-order being like us but greater and prior to us, and confronted in his day by the same problem that confronts us. If we thought about God in that way, as our predecessor and extra-big duplicate, it might well have made sense to imagine him also as having been filled with existential despair by the task before him. But it does not make sense, for God is not that kind of object. He did not long ago make a cosmos, which in modern times has unhappily fallen apart. No: the truth is simply that God's creation of the world really is a religious idea; that is, it is a mythic, archetypal, exemplary and inspiring model for our creating of our world. Just as the only world there can be for us now is *our world*, so the only god there can be for us now is *our god*. The world is ours; therefore its creator god is now ours also. The creation-myth in effect says, 'You can do it; here's how'; and the god functions as a guiding standard or norm.

In religious terms, the revision of classical theology that is needed now is not so very great. All we need say is that God indeed creates the world – but he does it in and through us.

2

This Day

We said that in archaic times the Sacred had immense power to generate ontological conviction. Wordy. I mean that the Sacred had the power to make people feel when they were before it that they were in the presence of something overwhelmingly powerful, authoritative, fearsome – and therefore supremely *real*. Also, because sacredness diffuses and spreads itself around, the Sacred imparted to many other objects and persons something of its own intense objectivity. Thus I am claiming that realism in philosophy, and also the ordinary person's sense of reality, is ultimately of religious origin.

Many of the leading concepts of traditional metaphysics – and logic, in fact – are just faded versions of religious ideas, though only one philosopher, Feuerbach, came near to understanding this, and the connections have not yet been unravelled in detail. In this particular case, however, the train of thought is straightforward, all the feelings being still fresh in our souls and easily elicited.

The idea of being or existence is the idea of something resistant over against me. It stands forth and in some way constrains me. I must reckon with it. It is not at all plastic to my will: rather, it inhibits me.

The first thing that has this ineluctable objectivity, and has it to the very highest degree, is God; but it also belongs in varying degrees to everything to which God has communicated a little of his holiness – which in the end means every finite being, since everything created has been touched by its Maker's hand.

So objective reality or being is ultimately nothing more nor less than sacred authority, and the more externalized, powerful and diffused-around is the Sacred in a society, the stronger will be that people's sense of reality. For there is no doubt: the Holy, over against me, is the most real thing I can ever experience and it gives reality to everything else. It is the source of the idea of Being.

People's sense of reality was therefore at its very strongest in the primary civilizations. In those days this present world and the sacred world were identical, so that to that extent there was no alienation. This present world was simply itself the religiously-satisfactory world, it was sacralized to the very highest degree, and people lived immersed in sacred reality. The art of Egypt shows what all this was like.

In another sense, however, the primary civilizations were highly alienated. They were the most complex societies hitherto achieved. This feat of social organization had been accomplished by expropriating politico-religious power and authority from the people themselves, and then concentrating, centralizing and enthroning it. The God was a king in a palace, and human beings were slaves in hovels. To make the city-state possible, people had had to surrender their own spiritual natures to the God so completely that the society was a totalitarian theocracy. There was plenty of sacred reality, plenty of being and objectivity around, but there was no spiritual freedom.

The protest that began around twenty-six centuries ago took a very odd form. The free, self-conscious and literate individual was appearing. He hated the spiritual oppressiveness of 'Babel'. He had to escape from it if he was to affirm his spiritual freedom.

The method of escape was subtle and powerful. The key move was to split the world in two, separating the everyday world of this present life from the 'real' and spiritually-satisfying world. This move at once devalued the world below, and made the sacred world a remote object of aspiration, a world above.

The teacher could now give vent to his feelings about this world. He poured scorn on the old politico-religious order, and declared that in this corrupt and fleeting world below there could be no real being, no absolute knowledge, no perfection and no lasting happiness. The whole of life was blighted by sin, suffering and futility. The only remedy was to escape from this world and seek a place in the world above, where alone eternal perfection and bliss were to be found.

In retrospect, the severity of the pessimism is most remarkable. All religious people became like the Jain saint, who is represented in art not as a human body but as a hole, an empty silhouette in a metal plate. The ultimate happiness that human beings seek had been pushed right out of the world of experience, and now was located in or beyond death. The believer pined for death. The Jain ascetic was supposed in the end to starve himself. The Christian also, as St Paul puts it, longed 'to be absent from the body and present with the Lord'. The sooner you were dead the better.

The two-worlds cosmology was most memorably worked out by Plato. Our world was a world of mere becoming, of flux, of phenomena, in contrast with the eternal and intelligible world above. Concerning this unstable world, no more than transient belief is ever possible: only in the world above can we find the objects of real knowledge, universal, necessary and unchanging.

All this meant that for two millennia, and more, religiousness was equated with the condition of being and feeling yourself to be an exile. All the norms of thought and action and all the highest objects of desire were located in the world above, and could be reached only through death. Real life started after you were dead. Human existence was rooted in the world above, and as long as you remained alive you were away from home. This world in which we are temporarily stranded is transient, unsatisfying and full of suffering, and we are very homesick. Oh, that the good Lord would take us – or that Death would take us, for God and Death are very close to each other.

Or put it this way: we now see that the ideas of an objective God and of life after death in a better world above are identical twins – in fact, they are perhaps simply identical, for they both set faith looking to something objectified, transcendent, unattainable for now, but which it hoped one day to come to. So it happened that faith became pure alienation, homesickness and nothing more. It never rejoiced in possessing its object; it was always pining after something remote.

However, though all this was true, it was never the whole truth. Everything depended on your understanding of the metaphysical status of the sacred world above. We have been assuming that it is taken to be ontologically more real than this present world, in which case we here below are indeed in a state of lifelong alienation. But the situation could be read in a quite different way. Plato was after all a *moral* philosopher. He makes the Good the supreme principle of his system, and locates in his world above all the norms for our thinking and our moral conduct. So perhaps when the images were smashed, and God was made invisible and shot up into the sky, he was made not into a super-being but rather into an ideal? Perhaps when the sacred world was hived off from the everyday world and made into a world above, what people were really doing under the mythical surface was simply making the distinction between facts and norms? Every young student who first reads Plato's *Republic* assumes that the world above is to the world below as the drawing-room where the quality live is to the kitchen below stairs where the servants live. He assumes that the two worlds are in effect of the same basic kind, except that there is rather more of this queer stuff called Being around upstairs than there is downstairs. So the student thinks, being like all ordinary folk a realist who thinks in mythical terms. And he is probably quite wrong. The world above is a world of values, norms, ideals; so try thinking of it as being related to the world below, not as reception rooms to servants' quarters, but as the principles of the internal combustion engine are to the engine that is physically in your car. The world above is not a parallel but superior and ontologically more 'real' world: rather, it is just a set of ideals, values, laws, guiding principles and abstract things like that. So there is no reason why you should let it make you feel an exile. And if that is the way things are, then the thinkers behind the great world religions, when they hived off the sacred world and projected it up above, were seeking to gain their own spiritual freedom by converting the Sacred from a dominating present political and ontological reality into a guiding ideal. They created some spiritual space around themselves by secularizing the world and idealizing the Sacred. This made room for change, and religion could become ethical.

Whether or not this interpretation does justice to what the classic world religions were saying at first, when they began, it certainly describes what started to happen at the Reformation. Christianity at last turned decisively towards the world. Metaphysics and monasticism were repudiated, and faith was internalized and moralized.

At the time nobody could possibly have said, 'This implies a non-realist or regulative understanding of the nature of religious beliefs', but nevertheless it was so. The faith was increasingly treated as inner software, an ethical guidance-system, a kind of internal programme for shaping what was now openly welcomed and enjoyed as a secular life in a secular world. In preaching, the sermon so deployed scripture and theology as to bring everything to a point that bore upon the will of the believer here and now, at this moment and in this life. It was called the 'application', and it meant that religious ideas were cashed like cheques at the point of moral decision. Even the funeral service now became chiefly an exhortation to the survivors to repent. Religious attention was no longer primarily directed towards life after death in the heavenly world above, but towards the old prophetic *Now, this day.*

So religion has returned to this world, after a detour that lasted for more than two millennia. Now the world is entirely secular, but the believer brings to it his religious idealism, and the world is sacralized insofar as the believer succeeds in actualizing religious values within it. The believer is no longer alienated from the religiously satisfactory world, for he is actually creating it; nor from God, for his action in striving to realize religious value and meaning within the world is identical with the creative action of God.

3

The Human Condition

What are we? Let us be objective, you and I, and look at ourselves as if from a public standpoint beyond the narrow sphere of our own subjectivities. What do we see? We see that we are biological organisms who live within narrow physical limits and move from birth to death over about seven decades. To one such being it may seem to matter greatly whether for him it is a case of two down and five to go or five down and two to go, but from the objective point of view such differences are not significant. We are all in the same boat. Every individual is alike ephemeral, and that is that.

What are these beings to do with themselves? They talk grandly of freedom, but they have much less of it than they suppose. The great social facts – above all, language – which have made it possible for them to become conscious beings with subjective experience, have simultaneously fixed tight limits to the range of their thought and action. They are able to communicate, and probably even to think, only by conforming to the extremely detailed requirements of socially generated communication systems whose nature they do not fully understand. They cannot break free. Even so heroically courageous, creative and individualistic a figure as Nietzsche, who was as bold as any human being is ever likely to be in rejecting society and tradition, could not do it. Though one of our greatest figures, he was also a product of his own times and he also had to work within the limits of language, just like the rest of us.

Seeing all this, Wittgenstein was understandably pessimistic and quietist. If the individual is finished then philosophy, chastened, must henceforth confine itself to recording social facts.

I cannot easily stomach that, so let us overturn it, and try to fight our way back to the primacy of subjectivity. While we were thinking about our condition in that so-called 'objective' way, we were not thinking absolutely. We were meekly accepting the terms of a socially-constructed public world view that was expressly designed to cut the individual down to size. Society keeps me in my place by representing me to myself as a fleeting episode in its long life.

It would be unphilosophical to accept such diminishment without protest. So I defiantly shift to the subjective point of view, and assert that as seen from within the field of subjectivity my life is boundless. I see neither its beginning nor its end: it is only from society that I learn of my finitude. From within, my subjectivity is a complete world that includes not only the relatively little that I personally do and undergo but also the far vaster regions that thought traverses; and the spotlight of consciousness, the *I think*, ranges over all these inner spaces like a god.

The *I think* appears to be what was meant by talk of our immortal soul. For if any feature of my subjective life other than this were to be immortal then I might well complain that its immortality is not truly my own immortality; whereas if the *I think* is immortal, then surely I am. So the *I think* is the immortal soul.

More than that, the *I think* of consciousness is very close to God. Especially on a Cartesian model of consciousness, the *I think* is as it were omnipresent, omniscient and omnipotent (or nearly so) within the field of subjectivity, for it appears able to range everywhere, with unrestricted access to and power over everything. For Cartesians especially, within the subjective realm the *I think* is almost an absolute monarch.

The affinity between the *I think* and God appears very strikingly in speculation about the incarnation of God in Christ. For in the incarnation the public and cosmic *I think* of the eternal Son of God added the occupation of one subjective world on to its other functions, and so became the *I think* within the subjectivity of the man Jesus of Nazareth. The divine consciousness became in addition a human one. Until the mid-nineteenth century few found much of a problem in this idea that the divine *I think* could simultaneously function as a fully human *I think*. Then the new historical and social awareness compelled some theologians to see Christ as, in Charles Gore's words, 'refraining from the divine mode of consciousness within the sphere of his human life'. The divine *I think* has thus come to be seen by Gore as needing to restrain itself somewhat in order to function as a normal human *I think*. Yet Gore continues to insist on Christ's full humanity, so it still remains the case that for Gore, as for so many others, the divine self-consciousness – if now admittedly somewhat self-restrained – can within a man simply operate as a fully human and normal *I think*. And this surely implies that in ordinary humans the *I think* is a kind of god within the self.

This is astonishing, and yet it is undeniable. Both a close analogy, and a close resemblance, seem to be involved.

According to the analogy, what the *I think* is to the whole field of subjective experience, God is to the world. Establishing a public and common world, society postulates God as the world's *I think*, who takes this socially constructed public realm for the field of his experience.

But the close resemblance is also insisted upon by all those introvertive mystics and near-solipsist philosophers of subjectivity; all those, in short, for whom the inner world matters most. For them, the *I think* and God are so close and so alike that their unity, even their identity, becomes something like an open secret.

Perhaps one reason for the very existence of society is that it, its public constructed world and its god, are required to check the *I think*, and to inhibit its tendency otherwise to solipsism, inflation, self-deification and madness.

The relation between private and public is delicate. The human *I think* is a premiss for arguments to God. It may not figure in overt proofs, but it is present nonetheless in a hidden way, for if my inner world has an *I think* to which it is present, to which it is subjected and by which it is unified – all elements of the self having a common relation to the transcendental *I think* – so correspondingly the public world also needs to be present to a consciousness before which it stands and by which it is unified and ruled. So the argument moves from the *I think* to God; and then, having reached him, it turns back with a new purpose. God and the public sphere, now they are established, must subordinate the self and subjectivity and secure their allegiance. This is done chiefly by a demonstration of the logical priority and superior reality of God, society and the public realm, designed to convince us that the subjective realm is derived and quite properly subordinate. Kept in his place, the human subject will not lose his head: but, by whatever means, that mad rush to solipsism must be checked. A Promethean affirmation of the primacy of subjectivity is dangerous, and God and society exist to counter-balance it. The *I think* in me cannot safely be permitted to see itself as alone and autonomous, and therefore as in effect being God to itself. It must be humbled and made to pray.

The theist humbles himself by positing the infinitely superior reality of God over against himself. The Buddhist cuts back the vain pretensions of the *I think* in a different way. He argues that our subjective world is much less coherent than we suppose. On close analysis, we find that it is no more than a series of states, just a row of scraps. The human *I think* cannot be much of a god if he cannot unify his own cosmos: in fact, says the Buddhist, we simply do not have the kind of unified and enduring substantial selfhood with which we would like to credit ourselves.

The debate that we have been pursuing never reaches a permanent conclusion. The self continues to be suspended between the pola-rities of society and nature, public and private, constraint and freedom, the individual and the group, and subjectivity and objec-tivity. There is no simply *true* representation of the human condi-tion: we are inevitably guided by the terms for representing it that are made available to us by our tradition. If a single truth could be told, no doubt philosophy would be enough; but it cannot, and it is precisely because the truth is not to be had that we find ourselves compelled to turn to the spiritual disciplines of religion.

Thus a third function of religion in addition to inspiring creativity in us and calling upon us to realize our values, is to give the self spiritual poise. A completely uninhibited affirmation of subjectivity leads to solipsism, inflation and madness; but at the other extreme, if the objective becomes too dominant it inhibits and represses the self. So we need a God before whom to humble ourselves, but he must not become so overwhelmingly objective as to crush us: he should be something like a transcendent but inward ideal that unifies the self through its allegiance to him, and prompts it to high spiritual aspiration, but does so from within.

An alternative way of achieving much the same result is the Buddhist discipline of nothingness. Egoism is kept under control by constant meditation upon the illusoriness of one's own self and the nothingness, or insubstantiality and impermanence, that pervades all existence. At first sight this particular style in spirituality may seem very different from theism, but in fact theistic mysticism – and also the Christian believer's dying with Christ – may include very similar themes.

Whichever representation be preferred, the function of our ideas of God, of nothingness, or of Christ's death is to stabilize the self, to hold it calm and poised in the face of the enigma of the human condition. Religion is our way of *making* sense of a life that otherwise would make no sense at all.

4

Man Alone

What we earlier called anthropomonism has a long pedigree in Western culture. In Christian art the heavenly world may be represented simply by the figure of the regnant Christ, or by a number of human figures, organized spatially by the painter in such a way as to show us that they comprise an ordered society. These images foreshadow a world in which there is nothing wild and, even more extreme, nothing non-human whatever. Only the human community exists, its world being generated by its worship and its social interactions.

Such visions of an anthropomonist world are frequent among Reformation radicals, anarchists and communists. The grandest, perhaps, is to be found at the very end of Hegel's *Phenomenology of Spirit*. All of them have a common ancestry in the Bible's visions of the new covenant, the messianic feast, the new Jerusalem, and the kingdom of God. And strangely, in recent times some people have come to see that anthropomonism is our actual situation, our whole world being made of signs and rules, our whole life being a continual receiving and sending of messages, and the rich and multifarious human communications network being itself the medium in which everything we can ever know or believe must be encoded.

Various terms are used to describe this insight: anthropocentrism, radical humanism and hominism (Fritz Mauthner's term). Some philosophers describe especially Wittgenstein's version of the doctrine as 'linguistic idealism', whereas we have used the term anthropomonism. There is only a slight difference of emphasis here, depending on one's angle of vision. From the linguistic side, naturally the language incorporates conventions defining human nature; from the human side, language is interwoven with our other practices, and is itself our chief tool for making our world.

If we had more intellectual virtue we would avoid such ugly labels as 'anthropomonism'. Wittgenstein detested them, and did well enough without them. In any case, the point is clear enough. Our world, the human world, may be seen in the image of a central Tokyo street in the late evening. It is a rich and busy network of highly rule-governed and symbolic displays, utterances and messages of every kind, flying back and forth ceaselessly. Diverse though they are, all human activities are expressive, symbolic and rule-governed, and so are in a broad sense linguistic.

Language comes first. Marvellous though natural science is, it is entirely dependent on the language in which it must conduct its business, frame its theories and express its results. Many scientists are most reluctant to see and accept the obvious implications. They prefer to think that language is so transparent that it can be disregarded, and that they can therefore directly test theories against objective extra-human facts. This however is not so. An experimental scientist merely tests on some point of detail the compatibility between the specialized language of a high-level theory and some lower-level language, usually the ordinary language that embodies our everyday world view.

As for philosophy, well, it's been said plainly enough by now that philosophical texts are just as much works of art, arrangements of symbols, as are poems; and there is no way of overcoming that character, which they cannot but have. The dream of reason, the fantasy of a use of language perspicuous, univocal, rigorous, compulsorily clear and unmistakable – was just a dream.

The nature of language remains in many ways a mystery, but it is not surprising that people doubt whether a realist view of language as somehow having the magical power to latch itself on to and to describe objective structures out there in the world is tenable, or even intelligible. In what terms shall we define the relation between language and reality? If in linguistic terms, then our definition will itself still be integrally a part of the world of language, and we will not have gone one whit beyond language. However many layers of meta-language we pile up, we can never cross the gap to reach that extra-linguistic [   ]. But neither, starting from the extra-linguistic end can we build a bridge back to the world of language. It is only social conventions that turn these marks I am making into meanings for us; there is nothing in the shape of the marks as such that ties them to other things in the world. Only social convention ties them even to associated sounds in the spoken language. Meaning depends on membership in a social group and on therefore knowing its rules, and on nothing else. Only social conventions strictly adhered to make it possible for me to express a meaning and for you to take it up and get my point. It is all social, and nothing but social.

And in that case, how can we have imagined that language might be used to travel beyond the world of language? How could some fragment of human communication turn up right outside the human communication-network and, this broken shard, yet be still a *communication*? And how can we who have by the human world been ourselves constituted as human – how can we, human, step out of our human world, and yet in doing so still remain human? We could no more do it than a spaceman could survive stark naked in interstellar space.

So, once the three ideas of humanity, linguisticality and of the public human world as a vast communications network – once, I say, these three ideas have come securely together in one's mind, then they create our distinctively modern kind of monism, a monism which in the new electronic age is going to be the general world view.

Even the memory of the intelligibility of the bare idea of transcendence is gone. Nietzsche, for once rather behindhand, liked to picture himself as dwelling in the Arctic wastes or as suspended in the void, but no such waste or void surrounds us; on the contrary, all ideas of outside are themselves of course very much inside. It is plain that there can be no jump-off-the-page, right-out-of-language trans-cendence, for we can only see sense in such an idea if in a fit of absence of mind we temporarily forget our own linguisticality. And by the same token Wittgenstein in some of his very last and most peculiarly deadly writing shows that there is no way of transcen-dence by hyperbolical doubt and scepticism, either. Descartes was just not thinking.

To do religious thought today we have to let this situation I have called anthropomonism sink deep into our souls. We must explore it all ways, for it is very strange and hard to get accustomed to. We are so used to the idea that in logic, in morality, in religion, in knowledge and in other ways human life is subject to extra-human standards. The reduction of them all to human linguistic conventions is highly disorienting. There is no longer any privileged Archimedean point from which the world can be seen objectively and as it really is. It is as if I live in a world without mirrors or reflections. How shall I ever get an idea of my own face? How do we get a sense of the human condition when there is nothing external to it, no superior obser-vation-point from which to survey it, and no standards by which to assess it except ones that have been developed within it and are integral parts of it? I feel acute dizziness and disorientation when I try to think the human condition in the light of the new monism. What religious response shall we make?

First, there is absolutely no alternative now but to identify this human world of ours with the religiously satisfactory world, to love it and to strive to realize ethical and spiritual values in it here and now. Hence the admirably sober good sense of liberation theology.

Secondly, not only are we forced now to synthesize the heavenly and the earthly worlds, but by the same token we must synthesize the religious and the ethical. The only act of transcendence now possible is the Three Hundred and Sixty Degree Turn. By a ninety degree turn I throw back my head and look up to heaven above, and by a one hundred and eighty degree turn I may turn about, retrace my steps, and seek to change my life. But the three hundred and sixty degree turn is something else again: it is a true panorama, our vision sweeping around the entire horizon until having seen everything we return to our starting-point, and look with fresh eyes upon the one thing needful: the neighbour, the next step, the present moment and the primacy of the ethical.

In this way the historic religious act, the act of yearning after transcendence, which in the past led people to seek God and the heavenly world above now brings them round full circle to the ethical. The religious turn was worth making, for it has shown me that the neighbour really is as God to me, and God really is in my neighbour.

Thirdly, we gave a hint in the opening paragraphs of this chapter that what I am calling anthropomonism, ultra-modern and radical though it is, may also be seen as a new version of millenarianism and biblical messianism. It is a very intense call to religious integrity. The old external supports, inducements, consolations, cognitive and ethical guidelines, guarantees and promises are no longer required. As all the religious opposites converge upon the ethical and the present moment, the whole spectrum of belief is synthesized back into white light. We have to unify divine and human creativity, the ultimate with the here-and-now, religion and morality, heaven and earth. Imagine a welder at work: the Moment acquires that white-hot intensity.

The corollary is that we must come to see as being relative the great distinctions by which in the past religion has been made thinkable as a distinct topic of human concern. If this is a shocking idea, it is also a biblical one: when the kingdom of God arrives, the Temple and religion are at an end.

APPENDIX

A Future For
Religious Thought

1. Religion without superstition

Keiji Nishitani is a Japanese philosopher with an exceptional knowledge of the West. He was a pupil of Heidegger, and has been a life-long student of Christian thought. Reviewing the long process by which the Western mind became progressively undeceived, a process that became complete in Nietzsche and Sartre, he has said that Western thought has now nowhere left to go except towards Buddhism – but it must get there from Christian premises.

It is a view that we nowadays hear often among people who are struggling to find a form of religious consciousness that is genuinely modern and free from illusion. A new kind of asceticism is emerging, as many of us react sharply against the extreme eudaemonism, the intellectual and emotional softness and self-centredness of popular belief.

Let me press the point: in the days when I was not yet quite beyond the pale and there was still hope of bringing me back into line, reviewers would urge me to be more 'positive' and 'constructive'. In part, this meant that I ought to be making more of symbolism and of the appeal to mystery: more obscurantism was being called for. But it also meant that I was being asked to give more confident assurances, for to my critics Christian faith consisted in a determination to believe, against experience, a spectacularly eudaemonistic popular metaphysics. In modern times, as wrath, judgment, hell, sin and holy terror have been played down, Christianity has been progressively converted into a comforting fantasy. The buyers have grown more reluctant, and the sell has become softer and softer. By now over much of the bourgeois Christian world, faith has become the purest superstition; for what is a superstition but a belief which is at once imprecise and gratifying, pseudo-factual and self-serving?

We who reject all this fly to the opposite extreme. We press hard a few forgotten themes in Christianity: its demand for inner truthfulness, its detestation of idolatry and superstition, its emphasis on the primacy of the Way of Purgation, its dislike of outward show and preference for everything that is austere, hidden, dry and subjective. We want religion to be a severe inner discipline without any consolations whatever. The colder and clearer, the better. There must be no more pixie-dust.

So we like Buddhism. It is a faith that imposes no duty to deceive oneself. It prizes scepticism and lucidity, and finds nihilism to be, not despairing and the antipodean opposite of faith, but rather, as refreshing as the blue heaven, an image of beatitude.

Exasperated, people say, 'That's all very well, but what do you actually believe?', as if it were somehow obvious that the more numerous, optimistic and definite one's beliefs, the better. Put thus, the assumption is plainly idiotic, and we reject it. What counts is not the magnitude of one's credulity, but the stringency and integrity of faith. Progress consists not in believing more things more firmly, but in becoming more fastidious about the line between faith and superstition.

As in the related case of sanity and madness, the ways in which people have drawn the line between true religion and superstition have been very variable, and are very revealing.

Originally, of course, it was simply the line between us and them. Our customs and beliefs seemed to us eminently sane and right and normal, whereas the customs and beliefs of other faiths were obviously absurd, impious and superstitious. This confidence was sustained by a whole battery of apologetic arguments, which at one time seemed sound enough.

But with the Enlightenment the old assured exclusivism broke down. Critical thinking was an application to all knowledge of Jesus' ethical principle of first taking the beam out of your own eye, for it required us to be as habitually critical of our own beliefs as we are of those of other people. Under this new and scrupulous kind of self-examination the old certainties quickly crumbled. The standard apologetic arguments were dissected and found wanting, and the authorities to which faith had appealed were all questioned.

The effect was to force people to draw the line between faith and superstition in a new way, not vertically but horizontally; not as a line between us and them, but as a line between that in every faith which is truly rational and universal and that which is merely local. True religion thus became 'natural religion', a small set of common notions, a minimal unitarian creed which supposedly underlay all the world's religions alike. This set of universal principles of natural religion was first formulated by Lord Herbert of Cherbury as early as the 1620s, and became the basis of Deism.

Unfortunately, the same critical spirit which had dissolved away revealed religion was speedily applied, by Hume and others, to natural religion. It was eventually shown that the principles of natural religion were not in fact primal, not universal, and not provable by mere reason.

So again the line between true religion and superstition broke down. Nor is it hard to see why. In the old prescientific culture of Europe, human reason had been thought capable of penetrating the appearances of nature and recognizing eternal verities behind them. Human reason depended upon eternal Reason, objective intellectual and moral standards which sustained all things. But modern science was born as the child of scepticism. From the first it implied that nothing underlies the appearances of nature except mathematical regularities. Reason therefore contracted in scope: instead of being able to recognize eternal reality beyond the world, it was now restricted to recognizing mathematical patterns in experience. The long-term outcome was that all traditional beliefs about invisible spirit beings and forces, their special concern with us and their influence upon the course of events, beliefs once undoubtedly part of true religion, now began to look more like superstitions.

One thing remained: even if true religion could no longer be defined in terms of a true objective content believed, there was still surely a difference in character between a truly religious person and a superstitious person. For a truly religious person is distinguished by a particular kind of purity of heart or integrity of will, a quality of unconditional dedication of his whole life, a sense of his vocation and of his life as a pilgrimage, which is unmistakable.

This new way of defining true religion has a background in the Lutheran doctrine of faith, but first began to be put forward explicitly in the thought of Kant and Kierkegaard. Because it emphasizes not what is believed but the way in which one believes, it centres religious thought upon the human subject, the believer and his act of faith, and so may be seen as part of the general movement of European culture towards a fully man-centred view of life. Religion and faith come to be seen as human and voluntary. Faith is a virtue, a disposition, an attitude to life, rather than a content believed. It is simply piety, and as such no longer presupposes any truths outside itself – which is just as well, for do we not all know that by now we have lost all the old objective realities, all the standards against which human beings used to measure themselves in order to get a sense of what they are and what they should do? We used to think there was just one everlasting and objective order that supported us, but now we realize that we in fact supported it. It was our own creation, a myth, one of many projected out in different ways by different societies. But with this realization – which has *constituted* the twentieth century – we find that the human realm with all its varied products and projections is all we have left, and we seem now to hang suspended in a void. Everything else that we once lived by is lost and we are thrown back upon our own resources.

But now, in this condition there is nothing left for faith to be except a free, voluntary and creative decision simply to choose a certain shape and direction for one's life. As a believer I just choose to live by and for these symbols, these spiritual goals, these practices, this ethic – and this, I claim, has to be enough, is enough, and in truth always was enough.

This new kind of voluntary and fully human faith is faith after the end of the old cosmos. There is no longer anything out there for faith to correspond to, so the only test of faith now is the way it works out in life. The objects of faith, such as God, are seen as guiding spiritual ideals that we live by, and not as beings. The very idea of an ontology is, in truth, one of the first things that critical thinking obliges us to give up. The world is not made of beings but of meanings, and religious meanings are purely practical.

The attack on objectivity in religion began with Kant and Kierkegaard, but it is only since Wittgenstein that we have dared to say explicitly that the whole of the objective, quasi-factual side of religious belief must now be rejected as superstition. All the old consolations go. Faith is purged of eudaemonism. Religious activity has now to be undertaken just for its own sake, as an autonomous and practical response to the coolly-perceived truth of the human condition. This is true religion: all else is superstition.

2. *Religion without dogma*

The idea that the practice of religion – its ethic and spirituality – can be entirely separated from doctrinal belief is not new. The Buddha first introduced it two-and-a-half millennia ago. His crucial idea was not agnostic but therapeutic. The Buddha did not just say, 'There isn't time to wait for theoretical answers to the great questions of life, so we will have to get on without them.' He said something much more original than that. He said, 'The very desire to ask the big questions, the itch for those ultimate explanations, is a disease of the mind from which we need to be cured.'

This doctrine of the Buddha's finally appeared in the West in the Dialectic of Kant's *Critique of Pure Reason*, where Kant showed how the desire for knowledge that goes beyond the bounds of experience arises, and why it is a mistake. That was in 1781. In 1818 Schopenhauer, a follower of Kant, was the first major European thinker to turn to the East. The movement from dogmatic to critical philosophy had opened the way for a changeover from religion based on dogma to religion based on spirituality.

However, these things become explicit only very gradually. A further step was taken by Wittgenstein, a follower of Kant and Schopenhauer, in the 1930s. Wittgenstein's linguistic philosophy can be seen as pressing Kant's Dialectic still further. By making us conscious of language and showing us what language is, Wittgenstein produced a radically man-centred and practical philosophy which aims to cure us permanently of the metaphysical impulse. And as philosophy becomes post-metaphysical, so religion becomes post-dogmatic.

Wittgenstein's new view of religion still arouses puzzlement and hostility, even among philosophers. In effect, he is a sort of pragmatist. Of religious as of any other language, the question to ask is not, 'What does it stand for?' but, 'How does it work; what job does it do?'. Language is just a human tool, and there can be no way of using it to go beyond the human realm altogether. All you can hope to do is to show how religious ideas work out in practice, within the human realm. And there you must stop. Religious doctrines are just 'rules of life dressed up in pictures'. Speculation is worthless, practice all-important; which brings Wittgenstein within hailing distance of the Buddha. He is also close to Tolstoy and other nineteenth-century figures who admired the ethics and the spirit-

uality of religion, while thinking the dogma oppressive and obscur-
antist.

Post-dogmatic religion is then not new. It has a history, and today
can be found in a variety of forms. It is, however, not widely
understood, and is certainly not sweeping all before it. If it exists in
the churches, it does so in the main in a non-explicit way, for it is not
yet tolerated as a legitimate option.

The reason for this is that within the churches dogmatic ways of
thinking have proved very tenacious. From early times there has been
a tendency to treat doctrines defined by official gatherings of the
hierarchy as being something like laws, and deviation from them or
failure to uphold them as something like a crime. No other religion is
a 'creed' in quite the same sense, in no other religion is there quite
such a strong impulse to use doctrine as a tool of power, and
nowhere else do we find people quite so besotted with the idea of
pinning ideological blame on their neighbours. To break with these
deeply engrained habits is not easy. People feel that without a firmly
guaranteed doctrinal framework they have nothing – and they do
not like having nothing. Notionally, they may be familiar with the
idea that the religious life largely consists in an attempt to gain
spiritual poise by habitually looking death and nothingness – one's
own death and nothingness – full in the face; but in practice they
want the very opposite of that. They demand that a colourful
doctrinal screen be erected to protect them from the void, and the
screen must not be tampered with.

There is a curious and revealing ambiguity about the status of
dogmas. They are advanced as truths, but when the going becomes
rough they are defended as rules. It is not enough for them to be only
rules of the club, for they need to be believed as truths; and to gain
some credibility as truths they must be entered for public scrutiny by
the same sort of criteria as any other purported truths. However, as
became clear recently in the *cause célèbre* of the Bishop-elect of
Durham and the virgin birth, one is not allowed to say that a dogma
has suffered refutation in free debate, and must now in consequence
be abandoned. If there is any danger of the candidate's failing, he
must at once be withdrawn from the examination. A dogma that
cannot be successfully defended as a truth is pulled out, and instead
declared to be invulnerable because it is an unalterable rule. Dogma
gets its appearance of unchanging content and its power of survival
from the tactical ingenuity with which people thus gain it a little

intellectual credit by advancing it as a truth, but then as soon as the going becomes difficult, switch to defending it as a rule. But exposure of the ambiguity is fatal. The tactical switch can no longer deceive us, and we recognize that when treated consistently as truths, dogmas fail; but when treated consistently as rules, they are of no intellectual importance, because a rule as such makes no claim. It is only a rule.

The extreme case of dogma-as-rule is the small authoritarian cult. Within the cult can be found all the strict unanimity and uniformity of belief which writers to the newspapers would like to see enforced in Christianity – and the result is of no intellectual interest whatever. The dream was that within a pure society there could be pure truth, uncontaminated by relativity, dispute or doubt. But the dream was – only a dream. A belief that is in the end not vulnerable to refutation by argument cannot be true either, and dogmatic faith turns out to be simply sociological, its tenets mere passwords. The influence of the community is so strong that it is easily able to ensure that all Christians, but no Muslims, shall believe in the ascension of Christ (and think of it as a truth for which there is evidence); and conversely that all Muslims, but no Christians, shall believe in the ascension of Muhammad (and shall think of it as a truth for which there is evidence). We take it for granted that religious beliefs are specific to communities, appearing to be intelligible and well-evidenced to members of those communities to which they belong, but not to others. And it is very striking that we do so take these things for granted.

Dogmatism has an all-or-nothing mentality; it suggests that unless you accept scriptures, creeds and the rest dogmatically, you must reject them altogether. This is absurd. When we have freed ourselves of the snooping, censorious and over-scrupulous psychology of dogmatism, there is no reason at all why we should not use the resources of religion aesthetically, expressively and regulatively. A religion is a thesaurus of meanings and values that can be used as we wish to shape our lives. Just as once you cease to be a fundamentalist you can begin to see what the Bible is about, so once you cease to be a dogmatist you can begin to see what religion is about. All its diversity is opened up to us and there is no reason why we should not, like the Japanese, freely appropriate elements of more than one religion. Religion is like art, only the material it works on is not stone or sound, paint or words, but just one's own life; and it is also like art in being purely human, though with intimations of transcendence.

People say that a post-dogmatic practice of religion is no longer the same thing: the original innocence has been lost. In the old days the mythic world was all-encompassing. It was the only world, we were immersed in it, and alternative points of view were unknown. But now we are like those Third-World tribal peoples who, after having had their traditional religion and culture destroyed by Westernization and Christianization, have decided to go back and attempt to recreate them. In such a case, is there not bound to be some degree of affectation or falsity? The taint of Western critical reason is indelible, and after it the Gods and the myths can never fully regain their former power.

True enough: but what about a case where the old religion was itself already pointing forward to this change, saying that it must come and is itself a good and necessary thing? Christianity itself from the beginning represented a drastic humanization of religion. God becomes man, the ceremonial is translated into the ethical, extraordinary charismata are given to ordinary people and diffused through common life, and God is no longer a fearsome objective Being but an indwelling spirit or guiding ideal in the heart. Above all, religion itself is no longer an external apparatus of domination, but an inner spirit of liberty.

So, at least, said the New Testament. But Christianity needs a vesture, and the Christianity we got was Christian Platonism, the faith corrupted by being allied with dogmatic metaphysics and embodied in authoritarian institutions. Because it is so light, open and sceptical the (broadly) Buddhist framework of the future is going to give Christianity much more room to breathe.

Let me repeat an analogy. It is sometimes thought that fundamentalist preachers take the Bible 'literally' and deliver the whole gospel; but that view is nonsense. In fact the revivalist preacher knows nothing of the Bible: he has merely projected his own dogmatism and his small-town prejudices upon it. To reject his world-view, and to study the real Bible by modern critical methods, is to learn as if for the first time what that grand, archaic and diverse collection of books really contains.

We extend the same argument to religion as a whole. When the distorting influence of dogma is gone, then we post-dogmatic believers, we 'Christian atheists', see as if for the first time what religion is and what it may be in human life.

3. Life after life after death

When the scientist Robert Boyle died in 1691 he left fifty pounds per annum for a series of lectures against unbelief to be delivered in a London church. It is significant that such lectures were thought to be needed: people joked that nobody had doubted the existence of God before the Boyle Lecturers began to prove it. Even more of a portent, the very first lecture, delivered by the celebrated Richard Bentley on 7 March 1692, was an argument in a new genre: an attempt to show that even if there is no life after death it is still worth while to be a Christian.

Boyle's picture of the materialist view of life that he opposes is worth quoting, for it shows what a clever man, on the basis of what he had read in Hobbes and a few others, could sense was coming. For these Atheists, he says without naming names, there is no God. They think 'that all about them is dark senseless matter, driven on by the blind impulses of fatality and fortune; that men first sprung up, like mushrooms, out of the mud and slime of the earth; and that all their thoughts, and the whole of what they call soul, are only various action and repercussion of small particles of matter, kept awhile a-moving by some mechanism and clock-work, which must finally cease and perish by death.'

Bentley, who was militantly orthodox and a hard fighter, goes on to make the most of the main weakness in that account, its lack of a strong theory of human origins. For us, that gap has been filled. Scientific naturalism has been our dominant world-view since about the time of Tennyson's *In Memoriam*, which shows a similar horror of it. We have in consequence seen a very rapid fading of belief in life after death, which has now effectively vanished at the public level of discourse and among thinking people.

Does this matter? Bentley himself faced the argument that since, on the classic Christian view, the great majority of people were scheduled for a terrifying judgment followed by everlasting torture, most people would be very much better off without life after death. On this view life after death, along with the fears of witchcraft, evil spirits, bad luck and so forth, is just another of those superstitious terrors from which modern science has mercifully delivered us. We can now follow Lucretius and say that death is nothing to us, no more to be feared than falling asleep, not an event in life that we will experience but simply life's horizon. Other people's deaths are indeed part of life and have to be coped with: hence the importance of our funerary rites. But my own death is not part of my life, and I can disregard it. I shall never mourn myself; and I have no more reason to regret the thought of a future without me than I have to regret the thought of a past without me – or even, to regret the fact that I play no part in the life of present-day China. Our lives are finite; so what's new?

Religious thought can seemingly cope, too, by following the Fourth Evangelist and demythologizing the Last Things into present experience. Heaven and Hell become states of soul. Each moment in life is a moment of crisis (Greek for decision and judgment). The Future Life becomes simply . . . our future life.

Can it be as easy as this? No, it is not; for something has been forgotten. It is no accident that the first major modern philosopher to come out into the open and expressly repudiate life after death, David Hume, was also the first expressly to reject the idea of divine or absolute knowledge that confers blessedness on the one who attains it. For in traditional thought death was a moment of revelation. Through it you came at last to a final moral reckoning by an absolute moral standard; you came to know the truth about yourself, and indeed the ultimate Truth of all things. Evil was to be finally conquered, injustices would be rectified, and the incomplete would be fulfilled.

But if there is no life after death, then the world has no *telos* or ultimate goal and nor have our lives. There is no big answer or final truth, and the evils of life will remain unavenged. We will never be any better, or know any better than we do now.

Here the break with platonism is complete, for Plato had oriented everything – knowledge, morality, the world and our life – towards one absolute and eternal *telos* in the higher world above. One may of course say with Darwin that human life on earth has a very long time still to run; but a long duration is quite different from eternity. According to our best current knowledge our universe, like us, will eventually merely peter out. There may be a rational case for interim hopefulness about the future, but not for the old kind of ultimate hope.

So we have here a very substantial challenge to religious thought. Two initial points need to be made. First, I for one am not very convinced by Nietzsche's idea of the Übermensche (unless one thinks that in a character such as Picasso we have actually seen the

Superman), nor by the seemingly contentless ideas of Nirvana taught by Schopenhauer and by the Buddha. Secondly, and more cheerfully, great art, a dedicated life, and love for one's fellow human beings are intrinsically valuable whether or not they are in some way endorsed by the nature of things. The loss of life after death is indeed an excellent inducement to disinterestedness, for it obliges those of us who wish to do so to live the religious life just for its own sake, and no longer with any pay-off in view.

Those points conceded, where does religious thought get its purchase now? I propose the Three Hundred and Sixty Degree Turn (a Japanese idea, by the way). By a ninety degree turn one may look up to Heaven above, or down to Hell below. By a one hundred and eighty degree turn one may turn back, retrace one's steps, and seek to change one's life. But the three hundred and sixty degree turn brings you full circle, after having traversed the whole horizon, back to the present moment and the next step.

Now let me vary the metaphor a little. Many people fancy that it is possible, in madness or mysticism or whatever, to enter a higher state of consciousness and there apprehend higher truths hidden from the mundane view. That is a delusion, but there is a truth very close to it. For as we return from the abnormal state to normal consciousness, we may see our ordinary world with the doors of perception cleansed and as if for the first time. So the real revelation takes place, not in the outward movement towards some imagined higher world, but in the coming back, as we renew our relationship to this world, and find in normal consciousness the religious unity of time and eternity, the inner and the outer, that we seek. After all our journeying the magic world of religion is discovered to be simply . . . this world. It has to be: there is no other. The realization is forced.

Plato sharply separated the world of eternal value from the world of transient fact. Christianity sought to link them, through the doctrine of the incarnation. But now that only our transient human world is left to us, we are compelled to identify them. The unprecedented poverty of our modern situation obliges to complete Christianity's project, and unite God and Man, mysticism and humanism.

4. *A struggle against theological realism*

In recent years a militantly anti-realist philosophy of religion has begun to be put forward in Britain. In spite of the indignation it has provoked, it is not going to go away, for it has deep roots.

Its chief source lies in Kant's idea of God. The main lines are well-known. Kant showed that God's existence cannot be proved, and that we can have no objective knowledge of God. God must therefore be regarded as an 'Ideal of Reason' whose content is largely ethical. As the rabbit by being always just out of reach keeps the greyhound at full stretch, so the God-ideal motivates the mind to seek the unification of our knowledge and the realization of ethical value.

In his last years Kant went further, developing the traditional attack on idolatry into an all-out campaign against any sort of objectivity in religion as spiritually degrading and superstitious. Religious entities must not be seen as anything but pure ideals. To reify them is to corrupt them.

God, then, is a unifying symbol of the goals of our intellectual and moral life, which is why the striving for self- realization is identical with the movement towards union with him. God is necessarily a 'my-god', bound to the believer whose god he is. Thus a person's god is a life-shaping ideal that he lives by, and has the same sort of status as a person's honour.

The human mind is a born personifier, and in these cases we often use personalized language. We say, for example, that duty calls, that noblesse oblige, that honour is satisfied and that prudence dictates. But we don't suppose that duty, noblesse, honour and so forth are 'literally' objective personal beings. They can't be, for if they were objective beings they could not function as our inward and personal ideals.

The same is true of God. In order to be God, he must be bound to a worshipper or group of worshippers as their own religious ideal, the goal of their lives, that towards which all their strivings are directed. So, then, to function as a god, God must be the religious ideal and cannot be an objective being.

In this way, by nudging Kant only half-a-step further, I developed in 1980 an argument to the effect that a religiously adequate notion of God must be purely regulative, that is, a guiding ideal.

For many centuries religion, although properly speaking it is an activity rather than a theory, has been set within a framework of dogmatic metaphysics derived from Plato. The metaphysics was so dominant that the proper nature of religion was buried and forgotten.

Belief-in was determined by belief- that; by which I mean that it was metaphysics that called all the shots. It defined the nature of God, proved the existence of God, gave to faith its certificate of rationality, told faith what it was, and then patted it on the head and allowed it to toddle off. Faith meekly took all this. It did not even protest when metaphysics added patronizingly, 'Of course you, faith, are a radically imperfect mode of knowledge, and in the end I will take over from you. For what you aim at, although you cannot know it, is the pure intuition of necessity, the vision of the divine nature. I will achieve that, after you are finished.'

In this way Christianity lost its own identity and was reduced to a comic-book version of platonic metaphysics for ordinary people. By and large, that is what it still too often is. The struggle against theological realism is essentially a struggle to extricate faith from this long metaphysical captivity. We are trying to purify religion.

When emancipated, faith is seen to be a disciplined, practical striving to attain a life-ideal that emerges from within our own natures. But all life is lived through symbols, and naturally faith utilizes in its quest the rich resources of scripture, liturgy and tradition. None of this is believed dogmatically, but any of it may be used pragmatically. We are quite free to make the use we want of the bits that suit us.

The standard objection is that all this is reductionist. People say that there is something fishy about this talk of discarding metaphysics. What it amounts to is nothing more than a declaration of intention to go on practising Christianity as a useful myth even though we know now that it is not actually true. Taking away the metaphysics means taking away the claim to factuality, and leaving only an ethic and a way of life. And this, say my critics, will not do. It is not enough.

For, they say, biblical religion is factual. Quite independently of platonism or any other sort of metaphysics, the biblical writers already saw God as the creator, sustainer and governor of all things and events. That surely means that God is postulated as a factual explanation of the facts of the world. Although at a different level, religious ideas as much purport to be plainly factual as do scientific ideas.

However, matters are not quite so simple as that. Look again at the old religious myths and doctrines. The divine creation and govern- ance portrayed in them are intensely ethical. The world order that God institutes is a moral order, and he is pictured as shaping events

towards the fulfilment of a moral purpose. So we are hearing, not
about how things are scientifically, but about how they ought to be
ethically. God is spoken of as Father, King, Judge, Lord, Shepherd
and so forth, and all these figures were in traditional thought seen as
having guiding authority. They lay down the law, they set the
standards and prescribe how things ought to be. And in creation-
stories we do not in fact find God inventing scientific laws or
assigning values to the basic physical constants. The order the
Creator lays down is not a scientific order, but a moral order: it is a
mythic portrayal of the way the world ought to be.

The upshot is that Kant was basically correct in holding that the
idea of God is a regulative or guiding idea, and that nothing should
enter into it that is not ethical. Rudolf Bultmann used to say, 'In the
Bible God is known only as Lord.' In plainer language, that means,
'The idea of God is imperative, not indicative; ethical and not
factual.'

Thus God functions in society as a personification of the authority
over us of the ideal order. God is, you might say, the moral ideal
mythologized.

According to a tradition as old as Socrates and the Hebrew
prophets, the essence of religion is the living of a virtuous life. If we
accept this, then we will follow Kant in regarding the non-ethical
elements in religious belief as superstitions, and we will seek to
develop a consistently ethical view of God. The struggle against
theological realism is then a struggle against idolatry and superstition, and for a religion that is rational and moral.

5. The second disenchantment

Around twenty-seven centuries ago there began a movement of
protest against the existing social and religious order, the Bronze-age
urban religion that then prevailed across the world from the
Mediterranean to China. The Hebrew prophets called it Babel or
Babylon, denouncing its gods as idols, its social order as a tyranny
and its sacralized view of nature as immoral. They were typical of
many other critics, for it was the period when the modern free, fully
self-conscious and literate individual was appearing. This new type
of human being was not content to live as his ancestors had done,
immersed in a sacred social and mythic totality. His aim was rather
to escape from it. Indeed, he went further, generalizing his sense of

oppression and need for deliverance to the point where he came to see the whole of human existence as blighted by sin, suffering and futility. It was necessary to escape not merely from the city but, astonishingly, from this world and this life altogether.

In the past people had seen the cosmos as the home of the gods. They believed that it was the gods who had built their city and had been its first rulers. But the new mood of disenchantment completely devalued the cosmos, the city and this life. People now said that here in this world there is no real being, no absolute knowledge, no true perfection, no bliss. All these things were to be found only in the heavenly world above. So the new scriptural religions became quests for salvation or deliverance; and philosophy, which was born at the same period, took the parallel form of a quest for transcendence.

In religion the aim was to escape from this world and gain a place in the heavenly world. There were some who held that the perfect world would one day come on earth, or that its blessings could in some way be enjoyed in advance; but for most people the heavenly world was a world to be attained only after death.

Because they represent what we have always been used to (and are bitterly grieved to be now losing), we may fail to notice how strange is the pessimism of the world faiths. They pushed the attainment of a religiously satisfactory state of things out of the world of experience altogether. The ultimate happiness men seek had to be located in or beyond death. All believers became like the Jain saint, who is portrayed in art not as a physical body but as a hole in a metal plate. They longed, as St Paul puts it, 'to be absent from the body, and to be present with the Lord'.

In the same period in which this kind of religion was taking shape, philosophy also began. The human condition had now become a formidable enigma. In search of understanding, the thinker strove to ascend to a viewpoint from which he could survey things as a whole and as they really are. The object was to escape from relativity and attain absolute knowledge of reality.

It has always been believed that to possess this absolute knowledge would make one blessed. The reason is presumably that if we could only see human life *sub specie aeternitatis*, we would at last be able to see clearly how it is fitting for us to live. When we see the truth and live according to it we will unite knowledge and morality, and so gain personal integrity.

More than that, our life will have at last become firmly grounded,

in a world more real than this one. The two-worlds doctrine, typical
of the perennial philosophy in general and of platonism in particular,
made a whole series of sharp contrasts. Our wretched world was a
world of appearance, of becoming, of flux, of phenomena, in
contrast with the real, eternal and intelligible world above. Concerning this world we can have only contingent, particular and shifting
beliefs, whereas the world above is the sphere of necessary, universal
and unchanging knowledge.

The effect of these famous doctrines was that for more than two
millennia people lived in this world as exiles. All the norms of
thought and action were located in the higher, imperishable world
and human existence was really rooted there, so that people saw this
present life as a condition of temporary alienation from their true
home.

Philosophies of this type were so dominant for so long that almost
the only religious thought we have ever known has been an
expression of homesickness. This world is transient, unsatisfying
and full of suffering, and we turn from it to express our yearning for a
better world beyond. Naturally, the relation of the soul to God was
modelled on the same themes.

The two-worlds cosmology began to pass away round the time of
the Reformation. More recent figures, such as Hume and Nietzsche,
are often seen as turning-points. But there is a case for saying that its
final loss has been very recent indeed. A typical symptom of the old
mentality is that intellectual passion should take the form of a hunger
for Being – and *that* particular sentiment persisted till only yesterday.

Again, we have only recently recognized that we have left behind
both marxism and positivism. They were both of them still
'theological', marxism because of its Enlightenment values and
belief in progress, and positivism because of its belief in an ordered
mind-independent physical world, a cosmos.

The 'platonic' era has truly ended only when we have lost every
form of the hunger for Being, every sort of realism and objectivism.
This has now actually happened or is happening, and it is the second
disenchantment. The question we have been raising, of a future for
religious thought, is in the end the question of how religious thought
can adapt to the new situation and become wholly post-platonic.

In effect, we have been trying to show that religious thought must
cease to be based on homesickness, must cease to disparage this
world and yearn for another, and must no longer pretend that

religious language describes invisible states of affairs in the higher world.

There have been some examples of what we seek. Think of St Cuthbert, or of a Buddhist monk, who lives in intimate communion with nature and is an ascetic not because he rejects the world but because he loves it. Think of Albert Schweitzer, who was so insistent that Christianity must become this-worldly that he fused the religious impulse with biological conation, will-to-love with will-to-live. Or consider again the suggestion that religious thought is a three hundred and sixty-degree turn that brings us back again to the human realm, in such a way that for the first time we see it as it really is.

Such are the lines along which religious thought must move in the future.

NOTES

Notes

Introduction

1. For example, David Cairns, *The Image of God in Man*, SCM Press 1953; revised edition Collins 1973.

2. Jacques Derrida, *Writing and Difference*, Routledge and Kegan Paul 1978 (= University of Chicago 1978). Good brief summary in Vincent Descombes, *Modern French Philosophy*, Cambridge University Press 1980, pp. 136–52.

Part I: A Life in Time

1. On the development of the idea of a history of Nature, Stephen Toulmin and June Goodfield, *The Discovery of Time*, Hutchinson 1965.

2. Charles Taylor, *Hegel*, Cambridge University Press 1975, Part One.

3. Neal C. Gillespie, *Charles Darwin and the Problem of Creation*, University of Chicago 1979.

4. C. C. J. Webb, *Studies in the History of Natural Theology*, Oxford: the Clarendon Press 1915, pp. 10 ff.

5. Lord Herbert's chief books are *De Veritate*, 1624, and *De Religione Gentilium*, posthumously published in 1663.

6. See, for example, Clarke's Boyle Lectures of 1705, *A Discourse concerning the unchangeable Obligations of Natural Religion, and the Truth and Certainty of the Christian Revelation* (etc.), 1706, for a typical statement of the argument. For Clarke, see J. P. Ferguson, *Dr Samuel Clarke: An Eighteenth Century Heretic*, Kineton: the Roundwood Press 1976.

7. William Paley, *Natural Theology*, 1802.

8. In what I have written, here and elsewhere, about the concept of Nature the influence of Roland Barthes will be evident. See his *Mythologies*, Jonathan Cape 1972.

9. Acknowledgments to my colleague Peter Burke.

10. For these paragraphs, see Charles Coulston Gillespie, *Genesis and Geology*, Harvard University Press 1951; reprinted, Harper Torchbooks 1959: and also the materials published by the Open University for its

'Science and Belief' courses.

11. Thomas Robert Malthus, *An Essay on the Principle of Population* (etc.), ed. Anthony Flew, Penguin Books 1970.

12. R. M. Young, 'Malthus and the Evolutionists', *Past and Present*, 43, May 1969.

13. Basil Willey's phrase: *The Eighteenth-Century Background*, Chatto and Windus 1940, chapter 3.

14. A. O. Lovejoy, *The Great Chain of Being*, Harvard University Press 1936.

15. Comments on these problems in Henry Samuel Levinson, *The Religious Investigations of William James*, University of North Carolina Press 1981, chapter 8.

16. For example, John Macmurray, *Reason and Emotion*, Faber and Faber 1935.

17. On these questions, see James R. Moore, *The Post-Darwinian Controversies*, Cambridge University Press 1979.

18. Charles Gore, *The Incarnation of the Son of God: Bampton Lectures 1891*, John Murray, second edition 1892, pp. 30 ff.

19. For an example of science-and-religion liberal monism, see A. R. Peacocke, *Creation and the World of Science*, Oxford University Press 1979. For an example of dualism, see Donald D. Evans, 'The Differences between Scientific and Religious Assertions', in Ian G. Barbour (ed.), *Science and Religion*, SCM Press 1968. Some useful materials also in Peacocke (ed.), *The Sciences and Theology in the Twentieth Century*, Oriel Press 1981.

20. I refer to the controversy over F. D. Maurice's *Theological Essays*, 1853.

21. Seeing this, Nietzsche also saw that the loss of the ideas of a better time in the past and a better time to come would eventually lead to the loss of the idea of linear time. Today the only remaining measure of progress in linear time is scientific and technical advance. When it stops, linear time will go.

Part II: The Mirror of the Soul

1. On the history of psychology, see for example W. M. O'Neil, *The Beginnings of Modern Psychology*; and Robert Thomson, *The Pelican History of Psychology* – both of them, oddly, Penguin Books 1968.

2. Friedrich Nietzsche, *The Gay Science*, trans. Walter Kaufmann, New York: Vintage Books 1974, para. 354. Good short account of Nietzsche's doctrine of consciousness in A. C. Danto, *Nietzsche as Philosopher*, Macmillan 1965.

3. William James himself is still a much better read than any book about him. I commend especially *The Principles of Psychology*, 1890; reprinted

New York: Dover Books 1950.

4. *The Varieties of Religious Experience*, early editions, pp. 160f. (The pagination of this book remained unchanged while it went through over thirty impressions in the first two decades of this century.)

5. *Varieties*, early editions, p. 505.

6. Ibid., p. 506.

7. In recent years a series of purportedly iconoclastic and revisionist books about Freud have appeared. I remain unimpressed by them, and urge the reader to cleave to the old Ernest Jones biography; to *The Freud/Jung Letters*, ed. William McGuire, The Hogarth Press and Routledge and Kegan Paul 1974; and to Freud's own published writings. Fine, intelligent interpretations of Freud are available from Philip Rieff and Paul Ricoeur; but for real excitement read Derrida's essay in *Writing and Difference*, cited above.

8. Breuer and Freud missed a discovery at this point. They failed to see the significance of the fact that neurotics function better in a language other than their mother-tongue.

9. Thanks to J. A. C. Brown, *Freud and the Post-Freudians*, Penguin Books 1961, for first making Freud's darwinism clear to me, many years ago.

10. Philip Reiff, *Freud: The Mind of the Moralist*, Methuen edition 1965, p. 355.

11. Unlike Freud, Jung was not very good at summarizing his own leading ideas. There is also the difficulty that fully critical studies of Jung are still rather few, and some important primary materials are not yet freely available to scholars. His long-term standing therefore remains uncertain. Good examples of the 'received interpretation' of Jung can be found in Victor White, *God and the Unconscious*, Harvill Press 1952 (and recently again reprinted), especially in the Appendix by Gebhard Frei; and in Frieda Fordham, *An Introduction to Jung's Psychology*, Penguin Books 1953. Today, Anthony Storr is the best-known sympathetic interpreter in Britain. As my discussion shows, with Jung even more than with Freud the main question concerns neither his scientific pretensions, nor his scholarly accuracy, nor his intuitive powers. Rather, it concerns the philosophical status of his ideas, and it has been very little discussed.

12. The available literature is somewhat erratic: it includes Bryan Wilson, *Religion in Secular Society*, C. A. Watts 1966; Michael Argyle and Benjamin Beit-Hallahmi, *The Social Psychology of Religion*, Routledge and Kegan Paul 1975; Geoffrey E. W. Scobie, *The Psychology of Religion*, Batsford 1975; G. W. Allport, *The Individual and his Religion*, New York: Macmillan 1950; Derek Wright, *The Psychology of Moral Behaviour*, Penguin Books 1971 (from the same author comes also an unpublished but duplicated and widely distributed *Review of Empirical Studies in the Psychology of Religion*); and R. H. Thouless, *Introduction to the Psycho-*

logy of Religion, Cambridge University Press, third edition 1972.

13. S. S. Acquaviva, *The Decline of the Sacred in Industrial Society*, trans. Patricia Lipscombe, Blackwell 1979, pp. 201 f.

14. Books about mysticism and religious experience are very numerous but almost totally uncritical. Try Frits Staal, *Exploring Mysticism*, Penguin Books 1975; Daniel Goleman, *The Varieties of the Meditative Experience*, Rider and Co. (= Hutchinson) 1975; R. C. Zaehner, *Drugs, Mysticism and Makebelieve*, Collins 1972; and T. R. Miles, *Religious Experience*, Macmillan 1972.

Part III: A Common Life

1. Eric J. Sharpe, *Comparative Religion: A History*, Duckworth 1975, is a valuable general survey.

2. *Essay on Man*, 1, ll.99–102.

3. David Hume, *The Natural History of Religion*, edited with an Introduction by H. E. Root, A. and C. Black 1956.

4. The first book in this genre that I know of is Chateaubriand's *Génie du christianism, ou beautés de la religion chrétienne*, 1802. That was the first step – to invoke aesthetic considerations so as to persuade people to look afresh and more favourably at *their own* religious heritage. But now I offer a challenge to the reader: who first, without any inclination to be converted by it, regarded a religion from quite outside his own tradition as *aesthetically* beautiful and moving? The point is important, because this way of looking at mankind's treasury of religions, as precious cultural resources, is itself becoming steadily more important.

5. Friedrich Hegel, *On Christianity: Early Theological Writings*, trans. T. M. Knox, New York: Harper Torchbooks 1961, p. 183.

6. Emotivism is discussed in all modern histories of ethics: see, for example, Alasdair MacIntyre, *After Virtue*, Duckworth 1981, chapter 3; and Mary Warnock, *Ethics since 1900*, Oxford University Press 1960, chapter 4. The equivalent theory about religion is discussed in, for example, E. E. Evans-Pritchard, *Theories of Primitive Religion*, Oxford University Press 1965. But it will be clear that I do not agree with the views of any of the above writers, and seek a more sympathetic understanding of emotivism.

7. For sociological theories of religion see, for example, John Bowker, *The Sense of God*, Oxford: the Clarendon Press 1973, chapters 2 and 3; and John Skorupski, *Symbol and Theory*, Cambridge University Press 1976.

8. The best short account of Durkheim is Anthony Giddens, *Durkheim*, Collins, Fontana Modern Masters series 1978.

9. On the great topic of the difference between Them and Us, see, for

example, C. G. Jung, 'Archaic Man', in *Modern Man in Search of a Soul*, Routledge and Kegan Paul 1933; Bryan Wilson (ed.) *Rationality*, Blackwell 1970; Ernest Gellner, *Legitimation of Belief*, Cambridge University Press 1974, chapter 8; Robin Horton and Ruth Finnegan (eds.) *Modes of Thought*, Faber and Faber 1973; Jack Goody, *The Domestication of the Savage Mind*, Cambridge University Press 1977; and Rodney Needham, *Belief, Language and Experience*, Blackwell 1972.

10. Basic themes of Lévi-Strauss's thought in two volumes published by Penguin University Books: *Structural Anthropology*, 1968; and *Totemism*, 1973. See also Edmund Leach, *Lévi-Strauss*, Collins, Fontana Modern Masters series 1970; and Leach (ed.), *The Structural Study of Myth and Totemism*, Tavistock Publications 1967.

11. Point taken from Vincent Descombes, *Modern French Philosophy*, Cambridge University Press 1980, p. 103.

Part IV: The Antinomies of Religious Thought

1. Bellah's paper can be found in Roland Robertson (ed.), *Sociology of Religion*, Penguin Books 1969, pp. 262–292.

2. Crude sociological theories of religion are to be avoided. But I believe the comparative study of different types of religion does reveal important analogies between the degree and kind of organization to be found within the pantheon, the cult, and social life in general.

3. Keiji Nishitani, *Religion and Nothingness*, University of California Press 1982. The most important recent Western book to show strong sympathy for a Buddhist outlook is Derek Parfit, *Reasons and Persons*, Oxford: the Clarendon Press 1984, but many other examples could be quoted.

4. Lloyd Geering, *Faith's New Age*, Collins 1980.

Part V: I Have Said, Ye Are Gods

For the title of this Part see Psalm 82.6 and John 10.34.

1. In the preceding pages the main allusion is to the philosophy of the later Wittgenstein – though it must be confessed that there are scholars who interpret Wittgenstein in a realist way. I do not: see, for example, my *The Sea of Faith*, BBC Publications 1984.

2. David Sylvester, *Interviews with Francis Bacon 1962–1979*, Thames and Hudson edition of 1980, pp. 28 f.

3. Ibid., p. 13 etc.

Index of Names

Acquaviva, S. S., 103, 122
Agassiz, L., 67
Allport, G. W., 221
Argyle, M., 221
Aristotle, 32, 34
Augustine, ix, 44, 65, 98

Bacon, F. (painter), 179f.
Baer, K. E. von, 35
Barbour, I. G., 220
Barr, J., 118
Barth, K., 130
Barthes, R., 219
Bauer, B., 65
Beckett, S., xi, 180
Bede, 115
Beit-Hallahmi, B., 221
Bellah, R. N., 153, 165, 223
Bentley, R., 207
Bernays, M., 74
Bloch, E., 163
Boswell, J., 104
Bowker, J., 222
Boyle, R., 13, 207
Bremond, H., 105
Breuer, J., 75f., 221
Brosses, C. de, 116
Brown, J. A. C., 221
Buber, M., 105, 147
Buckland, W., 23
Buddha, xi, 65, 69, 87, 163, 203, 209
Buffon, Comte de, 3f., 17, 20, 22
Bultmann, R., 212
Bunyan, J., 168
Burke, U. P., 219

Butler, J., 12f., 43

Cairns, D. S., 219
Chalmers, T., 31, 43
Charcot, J. M., 74
Chateaubriand, F. R. (Vicomte de), 222
Clarke, S., 12, 219
Coleridge, S. T., 65
Collingwood, R. G., 67
Comte, A., 120, 122
Cuthbert, 215
Cuvier, G., 23f., 33, 41

Danto, A. C., 220
Darwin, C., 6, 20, 25, 29f., 33–43, 48, 56, 62f., 131, 142, 162, 169, 208
Debussy, C., 90
Derrida, J., xii, 219, 221
Descartes, R., 5, 63, 91, 194
Descombes, V., 219, 223
Dostoevsky, F., 65, 107
Dryden, J., 115
Durkheim, E., 129, 134, 137ff., 144, 149, 222

Eliade, M., 153
Emerson, R. W., 71
Evans, D. D., 220
Evans-Pritchard, E. E., 222

Fabricius, 63
Ferguson, J. P., 219
Feuerbach, L. A., 65, 86, 105, 120, 129ff., 144, 182